CHICAGO'S MUSEUMS

A Complete Guide to the City's Cultural Attractions

•

Revised Edition

VICTOR J. DANILOV

CHICAGO REVIEW PRESS

Library of Congress Cataloging-in-Publication Data

Danilov, Victor J.
    Chicago's museums : a complete guide to the city's
cultural attractions / Victor J. Danilov. — Rev. ed.
    p. cm.
    Includes bibliographical references and index.
    ISBN 1-55652-135-9 : $11.95
        1. Museums—Illinois—Chicago—Guide-books.
2. Museums—Illinois—Chicago region—Guide-books.
3. Chicago (Ill.)—Directories. 4. Chicago Region (Ill.)—
Directories.   I. Title.
    AM13.C5D36 1991
    069'.09773'11--dc20   90-27049
                                                          CIP

Photo acknowledgments appear on page 283.

1 2 3 4 5 6

Published by Chicago Review Press, Incorporated,
814 North Franklin Street, Chicago, Illinois 60610
ISBN 1-55652-135-9

To my wife and colleague,
Toni Dewey Danilov,
an ardent admirer of museums and the arts

CONTENTS

PREFACE TO THE SECOND EDITION

Chicago is rich in cultural resources. Among its many assets are a world-renowned symphony, a highly acclaimed opera, a thriving professional theater community, innovative dance companies, superb public sculpture, fun-filled lakefront and neighborhood festivals, and a galaxy of outstanding museums.

This guidebook, originally published in 1987, has been completely updated. It describes museums and similar institutions in the Chicago metropolitan area. Once a handful of large institutions along Lake Michigan, museums have proliferated rapidly and now number more than 150 in Chicago and its suburbs. They cover virtually every field, come in all sizes and configurations, and are located throughout the metropolitan area.

Chicago's Museums is designed to acquaint you with the large and diverse museum world and to help you plan visits to institutions of special interest to you.

Nearly everyone knows about major museums such as the Art Institute of Chicago, the Field Museum of Natural History, and the Museum of Science and Industry; yet few are aware of their colorful histories, the extent of their collections, and the diversity of their public offerings.

This guidebook also looks at other major museums and tells you about the smaller institutions, many of which are specialized in nature or locally oriented. The information and illustrations are organized into three sections:

THE BIG THREE

Chicago's three largest and most distinguished museums—the Art Institute, the Field Museum of Natural History, and the Museum of Science and Industry—are described in this section.

MAJOR MUSEUMS AND SIMILAR INSTITUTIONS

Sixteen museums and museum-like institutions are covered here, including such places as Adler Planetarium, Brookfield Zoo, the Chicago Historical Society, Garfield Park Conservatory, Oriental Institute, and John G. Shedd Aquarium.

SPECIALIZED AND LOCAL MUSEUMS AND ORGANIZATIONS

This section reports on 135 other museums and institutions, most of which are smaller and more narrow in scope.

It is estimated that more than 20 million people visit these Chicago-area institutions each year, with about half going to the museums and the remainder to zoos, conservatories, botanical gardens, nature centers, and other such institutions. Some museum visitors take advantage of the Culture Bus, which travels to many of the museums on Sundays and holidays from May through September for $2.50. The bus boards in front of the Art Institute.

Chicago has one of the world's largest and most diverse concentrations of museums and related institutions, and the number continues to increase each year. The museums are a never-ending source of cultural enlightenment and entertainment. This comprehensive guide seeks to make these museum resources more accessible, meaningful, and enjoyable.

I

THE BIG THREE

Chicago is blessed with three of the nation's largest, best attended, and most distinguished museums—the Art Institute of Chicago, the Field Museum of Natural History, and the Museum of Science and Industry. They have far-reaching collections, exhibits, and programs in art, natural history, and science and technology.

Each is a leader and innovator in its field. The Art Institute is known for its Impressionist and Post-Impressionist paintings, Thorne Miniature Rooms, art school, and the diversity and quality of its collections. The Field Museum has a reputation for its lifelike dioramas, Egyptian mummies, dinosaurs, Indian exhibits, gemstones, and collection of 19 million artifacts and specimens. A pioneer in the hands-on philosophy, the Museum of Science and Industry offers exhibits ranging from a full-scale coal mine and captured U-505 German submarine, to Colleen Moore's dollhouse and the new Henry Crown Space Center and Omnimax Theater.

No visit to Chicago is complete without seeing these three world-class institutions. They often have spectacular special exhibitions that are highlights of the year. Recent favorites have included King Tut's treasures, Vatican art, and Tiffany glass.

ART INSTITUTE OF CHICAGO

Michigan Avenue at Adams Street
Chicago, Illinois 60603
312/443-3600

Hours Monday, Wednesday, Thursday, Friday, 10:30– 4:30;
Tuesday, 10:30–8; Saturday, 10–5; Sunday and holidays, 12–5.
Admission Adults, suggested $4.50; children, students, and
senior citizens, $2.25. Tuesday, free.

Rembrandt, El Greco, Monet, Picasso, Degas, Renoir, Cassatt, Van Gogh, Gauguin, O'Keeffe, Cézanne, Seurat, Hopper, and Toulouse-Lautrec are only a sampling of the great artists represented in the collections of the Art Institute of Chicago.

This awe-inspiring institution—with collections that span 40 centuries of human creativity—is especially known for its Impressionist and Post-Impressionist paintings. Among its holdings are Vincent Van Gogh's *Self-Portrait*, Henri de Toulouse-Lautrec's *At the Moulin Rouge*, and Georges Seurat's *Sunday Afternoon on the Island of La Grande Jatte*.

But the Art Institute has much more to offer: American and European decorative arts, paintings, sculpture, prints and drawings, photographs, textiles, and architectural fragments and drawings. The art of the classical world, the ancient Near and Far East, Africa, Oceania, and the ancient Americas also can be seen at the museum.

The museum was founded in 1879 by civic leaders and art collectors, many of whom donated their private collections to launch the institution. Among the leading figures in its early development were Charles L. Hutchinson, Martin A. Ryerson, and Mrs. Potter Palmer.

The Art Institute, Michigan Avenue entrance. (photo by Tom Cinoman)

Some of the prized possessions of the Art Institute are El Greco's *The Assumption of the Virgin*, Rembrandt van Rijn's *Officer with a Gold Chain*, Paul Cézanne's *The Basket of Apples*, Mary Cassatt's *The Bath*, Pablo Picasso's *The Old Guitarist*, Grant Wood's *American Gothic*, Edward Hopper's *Night-*

hawks, and François Auguste René Rodin's sculpture of *Adam.*

The museum also is known for its holdings of Chinese bronzes, archaic Chinese jades, and Japanese prints; examples of Greek and Roman sculpture in stone, clay, and bronze; European decorative arts from the fifteenth century to the present; American paintings, sculpture, and decora-

Grant Wood's American Gothic.

tive arts from the seventeenth century to present day; twentieth-century paintings and sculpture; objects from Africa, Oceania, and the Americas; prints and drawings; photographs; textiles; and architectural drawings.

Any visit to the Art Institute should include a look at the 68 Thorne Miniature Rooms, with elements of European interiors from the thirteenth century and American interiors from the seventeenth century to the 1930s. These intricate models, having a scale of one inch to a foot, were conceived by Mrs. James Ward Thorne and constructed in 1937 and 1949 by master craftsmen to her specifications.

One of the largest and most important assemblages of its kind in America, the Harding Collection of Arms and Armor includes all categories of weapons and defensive gear, such as suits of armor, equestrian equipment, swords, daggers, polearms, firearms, and other accessories. Most objects are European in origin, from the fifteenth to nineteenth centuries, with some examples from the Middle East and the United States.

One of the largest and most impressive additions to the museum has been the Chicago Stock Exchange Trading Room, the magnificent centerpiece of the 13-story Chicago Stock Exchange building designed by Louis Sullivan and Dankmar Adler. It was constructed in 1893–94 and demolished in 1972. Sections of Sullivan's elaborate stenciled decorations, molded plaster capitals, and art glass were preserved and incorporated into the reconstructed room in 1976–77.

The Art Institute also has the Kraft–General Foods Education Center, with programs for families, as well as an educational program that includes public gallery lectures, group and school tours, publications, and other activities; the Ryerson and Burnham research libraries; the Film Center, presenting a varied selection of international, classic, and independent cinema; and the School of the Art Institute, a professional college of art and design.

One of the city's favorite summertime dining places is McKinlock Court, a secluded outdoor restaurant surrounding a fountain in the center of the Art Institute. The museum also has other restaurants and the Museum Shop.

FIELD MUSEUM OF NATURAL HISTORY

Roosevelt Road at Lake Shore Drive
Chicago, Illinois 60605
312/922-9410

Hours Daily, 9–5. Closed New Year's Day, Thanksgiving, and Christmas.
Admission Adults, $3; children 2–17, senior citizens, and students, $2; families maximum, $10; children under 2, free. Thursday, free.

The Field Museum of Natural History presents the entire panorama of the Earth's natural history, from its beginning to the present. One of the world's great museums, it has more than 19 million artifacts and specimens in its collections and over nine acres of exhibits in anthropology, botany, geology, and zoology.

Founded in 1893 by Marshall Field and other civic leaders at the time of the World's Columbian Exposition, the museum first was located in the Palace of Fine Arts building after the world's fair. It moved to its present classically designed marble home in Grant Park in 1921. The landmark building was placed in the National Register of Historic Places in 1976.

The Field Museum is best known for its dinosaurs, Egyptian mummies, meteorites, fossils, botanic models, gems,

An aerial view of the Field Museum of Natural History.

American Indian artifacts, and animal collections. The story of man, the animal and plant worlds, and the Earth itself can be seen in the exhibits covering three floors.

The museum currently is involved in a $40-million, eight-year transformation of its exhibits and programs. Two major new exhibits—"Traveling the Pacific" and "Pacific Spirits: Life, Death, and the Supernatural"—have been added to the second floor. The first part of the third major exhibit—"Diversity and Survival in the Animal Kingdom"—will open in late 1991 on the first floor.

Some of the other highlights to be seen at the Field Museum include:

Ground Floor Eight dioramas and related exhibits on prehistoric people illustrate episodes in human cultural development. Another exhibit explores the mysteries and beauty of early Egyptian civilization, with coffins, tomb

The Field Museum's Place for Wonder is a museum-within-a-museum full of hands-on exhibits that teach natural history.

chapels, tools, decorative arts, and a facsimile of the famed Rosetta stone (the entrance to "Inside Ancient Egypt" actually is on the first floor). Bushman, the highly publicized gorilla that was a longtime resident of Lincoln Park Zoo, also can be seen on the floor.

First Floor (main floor) This is where the public usually enters the museum, coming into awesome Stanley Field Hall, with its huge dinosaurs, elephants, and totem poles. It also is possible to see a full-scale replica of a traditional Pawnee Earth Lodge dwelling and artifacts and exhibits dealing with Chicago region and other American Indian cultures; an African waterhole, the largest diorama in the museum; various mammals, reptiles, and birds; and The "Place for Wonder," an exhibit that enables youngsters to touch the tooth of a woolly a mammoth, handle a chocolate chip starfish, and pet a giant polar bear.

Second Floor (balcony) Always a favorite of visitors, the Hall of Dinosaurs is filled with fossil remains and skeletons of prehistoric mammals, reptiles, birds, and fishes. The space is dominated by the imposing skeletal reconstruction of a

Albertosaurus, the world's first dinosaur skeleton to be mounted with no visible supports, towers over Lambeosaurus, in the Field Museum's Stanley Field Hall.

mastodon, a mammoth, and a 72-foot-long apatosaurus. The "Plants of the World" exhibit contains 430 exquisite handmade botanic models ranging from simple algae to complex flowering species. One of the world's largest meteorite collections, artifacts and costumes from China and Tibet, minerals and fossil shells, the spectacular Grainger Hall of Gems, adjacent Grainger Gallery, jade collections, and "Families at Work: Strategies for Running Young," a new exhibit that deals with issues of parenting and ways that human and animal parents care for their young, also are on the second floor.

The Field Museum conducts basic research, fieldwork, and expeditions to add to its collections and our knowledge of past and present human and nonhuman life, as well as of the composition and evolution of the Earth and its planetary neighbors.

Participatory programs, classes, workshops, lectures, field trips, and guided tours are among the museums's educational offerings. Music, dance, and plays also are presented, frequently in conjunction with special exhibitions. Among the facilities are classrooms, theaters, stores, a library, and a McDonald's restaurant.

MUSEUM OF SCIENCE AND INDUSTRY

57th Street and Lake Shore Drive
Chicago, Illinois 60637
312/684-1414

Hours Summer: daily, 9:30–5:30. Winter: Monday–Friday, 9:30–4; Saturday, Sunday, and holidays year-round, 9:30–5:30. Thursday, free.
Admission Adults, $5; senior citizens, $4; children 5–11, $2; children under 5, Illinois school groups and Park District camps,

free. Combination museum and Omnimax Theater—adults, $8; senior citizens, $6; children 5–11, $4.

"The liveliest show in town" is what *The New York Times* has called the world-famous Museum of Science and Industry. It's easy to understand why. The museum is filled with hands-on exhibits and experiences that make any visit unforgettable.

The museum, which seeks to further public understanding of science and technology, makes museum-going entertaining as well as enlightening. Its emphasis on contemporary topics and concepts, interactive exhibits, and an informal educational environment sets it apart from traditional museums.

The Museum of Science and Industry is Chicago's number one tourist attraction and the oldest, largest, and most popular museum of its type in the nation, with an annual attendance of about 4.5 million.

The Museum of Science and Industry, south entrance.

"The Space Shuttle Experience."

A $50-million "MSI 2000" program, announced in 1990, calls for revitalized exhibits and public spaces, timely scientific programming, new educational partnerships, restoration of the museum's historic structure, and other improvements. To help fund the program and operations, an admission fee was initiated for the first time, starting in June 1991.

Founded by Julius Rosenwald, the chairman of Sears, Roebuck and Company and a philanthropist, in cooperation with business, civic, and public figures, the museum opened in 1933 in the renovated Palace of Fine Arts from the 1893 World's Columbian Exposition in Jackson Park. (The structure previously was occupied by the Field Museum of Natural History before that museum moved to a new home in Grant Park.)

The Museum of Science and Industry has more than 2,000 exhibits in more than 75 major fields in its huge 650,000-square-foot main building and adjoining new space center building. To see everything, it would take you several days. The best-known exhibits are the full-scale replica of a southern Illinois coal mine and the U-505 German submarine captured during World War II. Tours are conducted through both. Among the other old-time favorites are the walk-through heart; Colleen Moore's glittering "Fairy Castle" dollhouse; a full-size farmyard and barn; the world's largest model railroad; "Yesterday's Main Street," depicting 1910 Chicago; and collections of prized automobiles, racing cars, airplanes, locomotives, and ship models.

In 1986, the museum opened its $12-million Henry Crown Space Center and Omnimax Theater, which have become the most popular attractions. The space center exhibits—which show the exploration of space—contain the Apollo 8 spacecraft that was the first to orbit the moon in 1968; the lunar module on which the Apollo astronauts trained; the Aurora Mercury spacecraft; a full-size mock-up of a NASA Space Shuttle in which a 3-D film simulates lift-off and space travel; a replica of the first Sputnik satellite; and various other artifacts, replicas, and models.

The Omnimax Theater is a spectacular experience. A 76-foot-diameter, five-story-high tilted domed screen surrounds the audience in seats steeply inclined on one side of the theater. Startlingly realistic images, projected with an innovative super 70-mm projector, make viewers feel that they are in the film. Among the films shown have been *The Dream Is Alive,* taking the audience aboard Space Shuttle flights; *Grand Canyon: The Hidden Secrets,* where viewers explore and shoot the rapids of the Grand Canyon; and *To the Limit,* which explores the human body and its performance. The museum is producing a major new film on Antarctica.

Numerous new exhibits have been added to the museum's offerings in recent years, with many using computers. They include the prize-winning "Learning and Learning Disabilities: Explorations of the Human Brain"; the "Calculating to Computing" exhibit, which deals with the history and operation of computers; "The Money Center," which uses computers to explain the financial system and economics; "Food for Life," which provides personalized nutritional information through computers; "Technology: Chance or Choice?," which looks at the implications of scientific and technological advances of the last half century; "National Business Hall of Fame," where visitors can learn about the free-enterprise system and the accomplishments of business leaders honored in the hall; and an exhibit on superconductivity.

Some of the new exhibits explain the basic sciences, such as the "Grainger Hall of Basic Sciences" and the "Regenstein Hall of Chemistry," while others pertain to health, like "Healthworks," "The Heart," and "Conquest of Pain." A number of exhibits are concerned more with technological applications, such as "Wheels of Change" (automotive), "Earth Trek" (petroleum), "Omnicom" (telecommunications), "Civilization Through Tools" (machine tools), "Managing Urban Wastes" (waste management), "Newspapers in America" (press), "Gas Energy" (natural gas), and "The Energy Lab" (energy sources).

Among the other enjoyable exhibits at the museum are "The Circus," with more than 22,000 animated hand-carved figurines; "Architecture and the City," exploring the impact of architecture upon society; and "The Curiosity Place," an exhibit for young children.

The Museum of Science and Industry has a broad-based education program that includes science demonstrations, classes, laboratories, teacher workshops, lectures, library resources, and outreach services. It also has sales shops and food services, including an ice-cream parlor.

II

MAJOR MUSEUMS AND SIMILAR INSTITUTIONS

The sixteen museums and similar institutions that comprise the second tier of Chicago's museum world generally are smaller and more narrow in scope than The Big Three, but they all have exceptional collections and thrive among the leaders in their respective fields.

This category includes Adler Planetarium, the Chicago Historical Society, Museum of Contemporary Art, Oriental Institute, and Terra Museum of American Art, as well as other institutions, some of which are quite large and different from traditional museums. These include the Brookfield Zoo, Chicago Botanic Garden, Garfield Park Conservatory, Lincoln Park Zoo, Morton Arboretum, and John G. Shedd Aquarium.

In this chapter you will read about institutions providing cultural and educational experiences that are not available at either the three huge museums or at the smaller and more specialized institutions.

ADLER PLANETARIUM

1300 South Lake Shore Drive
Chicago, Illinois 60605
312/322-0304

Hours Daily, 9:30–4:30; Friday, 9:30–9. Closed Thanksgiving and Christmas.
Admission Free. Sky Shows: adults, $3; children, 6–17, $1.50. Children's Sky Shows, $1.50.

The Adler Planetarium.

The Zeiss Mark VI projector creates the star-studded night sky on the domed ceiling of Adler Planetarium's Sky Theater.

When Adler Planetarium opened in May 1930, it was the first planetarium in the Western Hemisphere. It also was the fulfillment of Max Adler's dream. In the 1920s, he felt the popular concept of the universe was ". . . too meager, the planets and stars too far removed from general knowledge."

When the Zeiss planetarium projector was invented in Germany in 1923, the Sears, Roebuck and Company vice president went to see the "artificial sky" and came back determined to bring the planets and stars closer to the people of Chicago.

Adler Planetarium still is the leader in the astronomical field, serving more than 700,000 people annually with its two-theater "Sky Shows," observatory telescope, early instrument collection, 5,000-volume library, and extensive educational programming.

The planetarium has three levels:

Main Level (underground) The Sky Shows begin here in the Kroc Universe Theater. The Robert S. Adler Hall of Space Exploration features the solar system in 3-D; a moon rock exhibit; transporter modules; and space equipment, models, and photographs.

Mid-Level "Seeing the Universe" features live video of outer space via hookup with an observing telescope in New Mexico. The telescope that discovered Uranus and a working optical shop (where you can sign up to make your own telescope) are among the exhibits on this floor.

Upper Level The Sky Shows conclude in the Sky Theater on this level, which also contains early scientific instruments and "The New Universe," an exhibit that lets you travel millions of light-years just by pushing a button.

The Sky Shows change every several months. Among the recent planetarium presentations have been "Secrets of the Ancient Skywatchers," "Focus at Infinity," "Ticket to the Stars," "New View of the Solar System," and the holiday show, "Star of Wonder." A new escalator transports audiences from the Universe Theater to the domed Sky Theater above. Special children's shows are presented at 10 A.M. Saturdays and Sundays.

The Friday evening Sky Show makes use of Doane Observatory, home to a 20-inch computerized telescope that, the weather permitting, provides live pictures to observing audiences. Images of planets, galaxies, nebulae, and the other heavenly bodies are projected onto an 18-by-24-foot area of the Sky Theater dome, allowing up to 450 people to see objects millions of light-years away.

Adler Planetarium has one of the world's finest collections of early astronomical, navigational, mathematical, and engineering instruments.

More than 2,000 people attend the planetarium's lectures and courses each year. Among the topics covered are stargazing, recent discoveries in meteorites, the big bang theory, modern celestial navigation, and the UFO phenomenon. The planetarium also offers the "Astro-Science Workshop" for gifted high-school students.

BROOKFIELD ZOO

3000 South Golf Road
Brookfield, Illinois 60513
708/485-0263

Hours Summer: daily, 9:30–6. Winter: daily, 10–5.
Admission Adults, $7; children 3–11 and senior citizens, $1; children under 3, free. Tuesday, free. Parking, $3.

Located about 14 miles from downtown Chicago, the Chicago Zoological Park—better known as Brookfield Zoo—is one of the nation's most innovative zoological gar-

Dolphins perform daily in the Seven Seas Panorama at Brookfield Zoo.

dens. Opened in 1934, this 204-acre zoo is known for its naturalistic and multispecies exhibits. It was one of the first zoos to present animals in barless outdoor settings similar to their natural habitats.

The zoo, located on some 200 acres in the Salt Creek Forest Preserve in the suburbs of Brookfield and Riverside, attracts about two million visitors annually.

Brookfield Zoo started with a contribution of 143 animals, 123 birds, and 4 reptiles. Today, no less than 2,000 specimens, representing more than 450 species, can be seen at this outstanding facility operated by the Chicago Zoological Society for the Forest Preserve District of Cook County.

Among the rare and unusual animals at Brookfield Zoo are the black rhinoceros, hairy-nosed wombat, Galapagos tortoise, snow leopard, kiwi, okapi, and Father David's deer from China (now extinct in the wild). The zoo is known for its breeding and conservation of rare and endangered animals from around the globe.

Visitors can see the gorilla family at Tropic World—Africa.

Brookfield Zoo has the world's largest indoor zoo exhibit—"Tropic World"—a full-scale re-creation of tropical rain forests representing Asia, Africa, and South America. The exhibit is 75 feet high and features realistic environments inhabited by a myriad of animals and free-flying exotic birds common to the region. Rainstorms, complete with booming thunder, occur three times a day in each area. Atlantic bottle-nosed dolphins perform daily at the popular "Seven Seas Panorama." Visitors may watch these intelligent mammals from the 2,000-seat area or through 8-by-8-foot windows in the underwater viewing gallery. Seals and sea lions move about in a seascape just outside the dolphinarium. In the Children's Zoo, youngsters can participate in the Pet Learn Circle or watch "Animals in Action" demonstrations.

The zoo's grounds include native burr oak woodland, formal floral beds, and plants suggesting the natural environments of the animals. Tree-shaded walkways crisscross the zoo, and a motorized tram gives narrated tours from late spring through early fall. A heated shuttle transports visitors throughout the park in the winter. Refreshment stands and restaurants can be found throughout the park. A well-stocked gift shop and a fine natural history bookstore also are located on zoo grounds.

CANTIGNY

1 South 151 Winfield Road
Wheaton, Illinois 60187
708/668-5161

Hours Museums—March–December: Tuesday–Sunday, 10–5;
December–February: Friday–Sunday, 10–4. Gardens and
grounds—daily until dusk. Closed New Year's Day,
Thanksgiving, and Christmas.
Admission Free.

"Cantigny" is the name given to the 500-acre country estate of the late Col. Robert R. McCormick and his grandfather, Joseph Medill, that includes two museums, 10 acres of gardens, and more than 200 acres of woodlands. Medill was a pioneering editor of the *Chicago Tribune,* and McCormick was longtime editor and publisher of the newspaper.

The Robert R. McCormick Museum is housed in a Georgian mansion that was the McCormick home. The building originally was a three-story white frame house with a wood-pillared New England entranceway designed by C. A. Coolidge and built for Medill in 1896. In the 1930s, McCormick added two wings—a southern portico modeled after Madison's home and to the east a replica of Jefferson's portico at Monticello. Then the architect, Willis Irvin, clothed the structure in red brick. In addition to the historic furnishings, the museum contains memorabilia and works of art.of art.

The First Division Museum, located in a separate building at the site of old stables, tells the story of this Army division in the two World Wars and Vietnam. Push-button exhibits, dioramas, audiovisual techniques, photographs, and a read-

Cantigny.

ing room containing newspapers, magazines, and documents explain the role of the division. Six combat tanks
representing types used in World War II, the Korean conflict,
and Vietnam can be seen outdoors in front of the museum.
McCormick, who served as deputy commander of a First
Division artillery battalion in World War I, renamed his
estate after the war to Cantigny, a small French village that
was the site of the Army's first offensive in Europe.

The 10 acres of gardens are divided into 17 areas, each self-
contained and focusing on various garden functions and
groupings of trees, shrubs, and flowers. The garden collections include roses, rock plants, flowering shrubs, ornamental trees, Douglas firs, alder, birch, ash, dogwood, maples,
columnar trees, lindens, and dryland plants native to dunes,
deserts, and timberline areas. More than 85,000 plants,
selected to provide color and drama throughout the year, are
grown annually in Cantigny's greenhouses for display in the
gardens.

You are welcome to picnic on Cantigny's grounds, and campgrounds are available to organized youth groups. Sunday afternoon concerts, mostly chamber music, are held at 3 P.M. (except January) in the library of the McCormick Museum. Reservations are required for the concerts.

CHICAGO ACADEMY OF SCIENCES

2001 North Clark Street
Chicago, Illinois 60614
312/549-0606

Hours Daily, 10–5. Closed Christmas.
Admission Adults, $1; children 6–17, students, and senior citizens, 50¢. Monday, free.

The Chicago Academy of Sciences, the oldest science museum in the Midwest, was founded in 1857. It originally concentrated on the natural habitat of the metropolitan area, but now its offerings cover all aspects of natural history.

The academy is located in Lincoln Park on the city's North Side, across the street from the Lincoln Park Zoo. Although

Chicago Academy of Sciences.

A mammal's body covering can help it hide, protect it from thorns and biting animals, or make it dangerous to touch. This box has a mammal example of each of these body cover-ups.

"Stencils," "Clam-up," and the "Great Mammal Cover-up" are a few of the discover boxes children can examine in the Children's Gallery at the Chicago Academy of Sciences.

a relatively small institution, it has three floors of colorful exhibits that make extensive use of lifelike dioramas and displays incorporating birds, mammals, insects, reptiles, fish, and amphibians into natural settings.

You can start with a visit to the past, through a coal forest that shows the Chicago area of 300 million years ago, and then travel down a grassy path past a replica of Starved Rock Canyon. It is like an indoor field trip through the past and present natural areas of the Great Lakes region. Walk-through exhibits depicting the island biology of Galapagos and New Zealand and changing exhibits on current environmental issues can be found on the third floor. The museum also has a Children's Gallery that features live animals, fossils, artifacts, and rocks for children to explore.

The academy offers weekend workshops and events for children and adults, field trips to local wilderness preserves, lectures on environmental and scientific issues, daily nature videos in the Conservation Theater, special family programs, and conferences that bring scientific experts together for research and education.

CHICAGO BOTANIC GARDEN

Lake-Cook Road and Edens Expressway
Glencoe, Illinois 60022
708/835-5440

Hours Daily, 8–sunset.
Admission Free.

The Chicago Botanic Garden is an example of how a neglected, polluted, insect-infested swamp can be transformed into a 300-acre environmental showcase with a picturesque lake, beautiful gardens, stately trees, and abundant wildlife. All of this has happened since 1965, when the Forest Preserve District of Cook County and Chicago Horticultural Society joined forces to develop this natural habitat in suburban Glencoe.

The botanic garden, operated as part of the Forest Preserve District and managed by the Chicago Horticultural Society, offers visitors a year-round educational experience with its gardens, greenhouses, exhibits, demonstrations, nature trails, lectures, classes, and more.

Among the major display gardens are the Krasberg Rose Garden, Regenstein Fruit and Vegetable Garden, Sansho-En Japanese Garden Islands, Heritage Garden, Landscape Demonstration Gardens, Prairie Development Area, and special learning gardens for the disabled and visually impaired. The prairie area is an ongoing restoration project with samplings of wildflowers and grasses from the Midwest.

A 15-acre section known as Turnbull Woods has winding nature trails with labeled plants. This conservation area contains plants native to the Great Lakes region.

The Education Center is the focal point of the botanic

The Regenstein Fruit and Vegetable Garden at Chicago Botanic Garden.

garden, with 10 display greenhouses, an exhibit hall with changing shows, a museum and library, classrooms and auditorium, and gift shop and restaurant. Narrated tram tours of the grounds also depart from the center all year long.

From eight to ten art exhibitions of a botanical nature are presented annually, as well as displays of plant materials and a permanent interactive exhibit titled "The Plant-People Partnership." The educational services include courses in botany and horticulture, botanical crafts, lectures, and group tours.

The Botanic Garden also conducts research. Two major current projects are the evaluation of plant materials from Japan and the Soviet Union, and the development of a cooperative plant introduction program called "Chicago-land Grows," with the Ornamental Growers Association of Northern Illinois and the Morton Arboretum.

Chicago's first locomotive, the "Pioneer."

CHICAGO HISTORICAL SOCIETY

Clark Street at North Avenue
Chicago, Illinois 60614
312/642-4600

Hours Exhibition galleries—Monday–Saturday, 9:30–4:30;
Sunday, 12–5. Research collections—Tuesday–Saturday,
9:30–4:30. Closed New Year's Day, Thanksgiving, and Christmas.
Suggested admission Adults, $3; students 17–22 and senior
citizens, $2; children 6–17, $1. Monday, free.

These wraps, circa 1908, are exhibited in the Costume Gallery.

Founded in 1856, the Chicago Historical Society has the distinction of being Chicago's oldest cultural institution. The museum is a fascinating storehouse of exhibits, collections, and other materials relating to the history of Chicago and Illinois.

The Chicago history gallery contains many artifacts pertaining to the founding and development of the city, including the first settlers and Indians, Fort Dearborn, the Chicago Fire of 1871, the World's Columbian Exposition of 1893, and Chicago's growth during the twentieth century. The story of the 1871 fire that devastated much of the city is shown through animated exhibits. Chicago's first fire engine and first locomotive, the "Pioneer," are favorites among the museum's 200,000 annual visitors.

The Illinois Pioneer Life Gallery features full–size replicas of an early kitchen, living room, and barn with farm implements. Volunteers in period dress frequently demonstrate skills used in daily life, such as candle dipping, grain winnowing, spinning, and weaving.

Among the other exhibits at the museum are "We The People: Creating a New Nation," which features the printing of the Declaration of Independence; "A House Divided: America in the Age of Lincoln," a Civil War exhibit; a series of biennial exhibitions, titled "Prologue to a New Century"; and an exhibit on Chicago's contributions to American life in areas such as reform, architecture, city planning, merchandising, culture, and literature.

The Chicago Historical Society also has an extensive research library, collections, and archives that include rare books, manuscripts, prints, photographs, architectural drawings, city directories, and genealogical information. The museum completed a $15-million renovation and expansion program in 1988.

CHICAGO PUBLIC LIBRARY CULTURAL CENTER

78 East Washington Street
Chicago, Illinois 60602
312/744-6630 (Chicago Office of Fine Arts)
312/269-2820 (Cultural Center office)
312/346-3278 (for information about exhibits and programs)

Hours Monday–Thursday, 9–7; Friday, 9–6; Saturday, 9–5.
Closed holidays and Sundays except for scheduled programs.
Admission Free.

Each year the Chicago Office of Fine Arts, Department of Cultural Affairs, and the Chicago Public Library present

Preston Bradley Hall, the Chicago Public Library Cultural Center.

some 500 cultural events free of charge at Chicago's former central library—now known as the Cultural Center.

The exhibits, offered in the landmark building's four galleries, deal with painting, sculpture, photography, graphics, crafts, architecture, and design. They range from one-person shows by local artists to international traveling exhibitions.

The programs, which are presented almost daily at 12:15 and 5:30 P.M., feature music, dance, theater, literary arts, and films. Lectures, seminars, demonstrations, workshops, and conferences also are held at the Cultural Center.

The Cultural Center continues to serve as a major library facility.

The fourth floor exhibit hall at the Cultural Center. (photo by Cheryl Tadin)

GARFIELD PARK CONSERVATORY

300 North Central Park Boulevard
Chicago, Illinois 60624
312/533-1281

Hours Daily, 9–5. During flower shows—daily, 10–6, and
Friday, 9–9.
Admission Free.

The Chicago Park District operates major conservatories in
Garfield and Lincoln parks. Built in 1893, the landmark
Garfield Park Conservatory houses one of the most beautiful
publicly owned botanical gardens under glass in the world.
It offers more than 5,000 species and varieties of plants,
many of which are unusual and exotic.

The conservatory covers 4½ acres and includes hot beds,

cold frames, and propagating houses, where 300,000 plants are shown each year, including those used in Park District floral shows. Major attractions at the Garfield Park Conservatory are:

Palm House A tropical paradise of graceful palms and many varieties of exotic foliage plants can be seen in this 85-by-250-foot building. Among the highlights are date, coconut, Chinese fan, Scheelea leandroana, Carnauba wax, and double coconut palms.

Aroid House More exotic plants grow in the humid, tropical environment of the Aroid House. You can see many species of philodendron vines and colorful leaves of caladium, hypoestes, hoya, and columnea.

The Fernery About 100 types of ferns from the tropical forest are displayed in this house, daubed against striated rocks surrounding a waterfall and pool.

Cactus House One of the nation's finest cactus displays includes 85 genera and 400 species and varieties presented in a Southwestern desert setting.

Horticultural Hall and Show House The Horticultural Hall is one of the world's largest exhibition halls. The Show House got its name from its exceptional displays of foliage and flowering plants. Four major shows are held here annually: azalea, camellia, and rhododendron in February; lilies and other bulbous plants around Easter; chrysanthemum during November; and poinsettias and ornamental peppers, cabbage, and snow bush at Christmas.

Warm and Economic Houses A variety of tropical plants noted for their economic value in fruit, timber, essential oils, perfume, and spices such as fig trees, cacao, Queensland nut, papaya, and annato are displayed here.

Free guided tours are available for schools and organizations by appointment. Trained personnel also are available to answer questions on house plants and gardening in general by calling 533-1281.

LINCOLN PARK CONSERVATORY

2400 North Stockton Drive at Fullerton Parkway
Chicago, Illinois 60614
312/294-4770

Hours Daily, 9–5. During show hours—daily, 10–6; Friday, 9–9.
Admission Free.

The Lincoln Park Conservatory—one of two such facilities operated by the Chicago Park District—ranks among the finest and most popular in the world. More than half a million people annually come to see its impressive collection of exotic plants and trees and ever-changing floral exhibits.

Built in 1891–92, the conservatory consists of four huge glassed buildings, 18 propagating houses, cold frames, and hot beds, covering three acres adjacent to the zoo in Lincoln Park on Chicago's North Side.

The contents of four major buildings include:

Palm House A 50-foot fiddle-leaf rubber tree from Africa is the prime attraction here. The building also contains a fish-tail palm from India that produces wine, a group of sentry palms once used in thatching, tapioca and fig trees, a number of ornamental palms, rare orchids, and a large collection of tropical and subtropical flora.

Fernery This is a jewel-like sunken glade in a tropical setting. The cycads, oldest plant in the conservatory, can be seen here. They are an intermediate link between flowering plants and such flowerless plants as ferns and mosses.

Cactus House The old Tropical House has been renovated and converted into a showcase for many varieties of cacti and succulents from the Americas and South Africa.

Show House Four major shows are presented annually (concurrently with those at the Garfield Park Conservatory):

Lincoln Park Conservatory.

azaleas during February and early March, Easter flowers in the spring, chrysanthemums in November, and Christmas flowers during the holiday season. Fancy-leaved caladiums, rex begonias, crotons, and other foliage plants are displayed in the building during the summer.

Two large gardens also can be seen outside the conservatory: the Main Garden, with eight formal beds covering nearly a square block, and Grandmother's Garden, containing informal beds of perennial and other flowers.

LINCOLN PARK ZOO

2200 North Cannon Drive
Chicago, Illinois 60614
312/294-4660

Hours Daily, 9–5.
Admission Free.

Lincoln Park Zoo began in 1868 with a gift of a pair of swans. It now has one of the nation's largest animal collections, with more than 2,200 exotic and endangered mammals, birds, and reptiles from throughout the world.

Operated by the Chicago Park District and assisted by the Lincoln Park Zoological Society, the 35-acre zoo in the heart of Chicago has an annual attendance of over four million. One of the first urban zoos, it continues to be among the most popular.

A recent multimillion-dollar renovation and expansion program integrates state-of-the-art naturalistic habitats with landmark structures. Among the new facilities are a Large Mammal Area, Antelope and Zebra Area, Penguin and Seabird House, and Great Ape House. The longstanding Lion, Primate, and Bird Houses, as well as the Children's Zoo, also have been renovated as part of the master plan.

Lincoln Park Zoo has one of the finest collections of primates anywhere, with the emphasis being on marmosets, lemurs, and great apes. The Great Ape House is regarded as a model home for gorilla, chimpanzee, and orangutan family groups.

The Large Mammal Area is a four-acre home for hippos, rhinos, elephants, giraffes, wolves, and bears, while the Antelope and Zebra Area provides a similar-sized pastoral

Snuggling elephants at the Lincoln Park Zoo. (photo by Susan Reich)

oasis for zebras, bison, camels, and a variety of African antelope.

The Penguin and Seabird House is a climate-controlled environment with large swimming pools for various types of penguins and seabirds. Among the other principal offerings are the Sea Lion Pool; Bird House; Small Mammal House, with its nocturnal area; Crown-Field Center, featuring koalas; Children's Zoo and Nursery; and Farm-in-the-Zoo, a five- acre replica of a working midwestern farm with horses, cows, and other farm animals.

Lincoln Park Zoo is committed to preserving endangered species and serves as a resource for education and conservation that reaches far beyond Chicago and Illinois. Information about tours, classes, and special programs can be obtained at the Crown-Field Center.

MORTON ARBORETUM

Route 53
Lisle, Illinois 60532
708/968-0074

Hours Grounds—May–October: daily, 9–7. November–April: daily, 9–5. Visitor Center—daily, 9–5. Administration Building—Monday–Friday, 9–5. Library—Monday–Friday, 9–5. Saturday, 10–4. Herbarium by appointment. Closed holidays.
Admission Per car, $3.

The 1,500-acre Morton Arboretum is a "living museum" with extensive collections of growing trees, shrubs, and vines displayed outdoors for the study and enjoyment of the public. It is located just north of Lisle at the intersection of Route 53 and the East-West Tollway.

The arboretum was established in 1922 by Joy Morton, founder of the Morton Salt Company, on the grounds of his DuPage County estate. His lifelong interest in trees was inherited from his father, J. Sterling Morton, who originated Arbor Day.

The arboretum was created to collect woody plants from around the world and evaluate their horticultural suitability for northeastern Illinois, to help the public know and use good ornamental trees and shrubs, and to further public understanding of the natural history and ecology of the native landscape.

Developed on land once used for agricultural crops and grazing, the arboretum has sizable tracts of woodland that have been relatively undisturbed since 1922, as well as areas where cultivated woody plants have been introduced. More than 4,800 kinds of trees and shrubs can be seen at the horticultural center.

The plants are of two types as to origin—native plants indigenous to the area and introduced plants from elsewhere. The native plants are found mainly in the natural areas, especially woodlands and wetlands. Cultivated collections require more care and are of four types: botanical groups, plants that are related, like the maple collection; landscape groups, plants having a similar use, such as the

Lake Marmo and vicinity, part of the Morton Arboretum. (photo by John Kohout)

hedge collection; geographic groups, plants with a common place of origin, like the Japanese collection; and association groups, plants that occur together in natural plant communities, such as the prairie restoration.

Most visits to Morton Arboretum begin at the Visitor Center and the adjacent Information Building, which contains exhibits. You may tour the grounds with your car (it takes about an hour to cover the nearly eight-mile route) or take one of four hiking paths through the woods. Special facilities include a theater offering full introductory audiovisual programs; new Research Center facilities; the Herbarium, a collection of dried, pressed plant specimens; and research laboratories. The Plant Clinic offers help with plant identification, diagnosis of woody plant ailments, and selection of plants for landscaping. The Sterling Morton Library holds thousands of books on botany, natural history, horticulture, landscape architecture, and related subjects.

MUSEUM OF CONTEMPORARY ART

237 East Ontario Street
Chicago, Illinois 60611
312/280-2660

Hours Tuesday–Saturday, 10–5; Sunday and holidays, 12–5. Closed New Year's Day, Thanksgiving, and Christmas.
Admission Suggested donations—adults, $3; senior citizens, students, and children under 16, $2. Tuesday, free.

The Museum of Contemporary Art was founded in 1967 to provide a showcase for twentieth-century art with an emphasis on postwar and contemporary art. Known for its unusual and provocative collections and exhibitions, it often features prominent and emerging artists experimenting with new media and concepts.

Museum of Contemporary Art.

In 1988, the museum announced its intention to relocate to the site of the Chicago Avenue Armory to build a new museum and sculpture garden. The new facility will have from 100,000 to 125,000 square feet with space for expanding collections, exhibitions, and educational and cultural programs. It is scheduled to open in 1995.

Located on Chicago's Near North Side, the museum frequently presents exhibitions beyond the visitors' usual artistic encounters, such as an exhibit in which Vito Acconci used his body to create works of art and when the entire building was wrapped like a huge package by Christo to achieve his vision. It was Christo's first project in the United States.

Areas of concentration in the museum's permanent collections are surrealism, earthart, pop art/nouveau realism, and Chicago artists from 1950 to the present. Local, national, and international artists are represented.

The Museum of Contemporary Art has collected key examples of the three "generations" of presently recognized Chicago artists—monster roster (Leon Golub, for example), imagism (*e.g.*, Jim Nutt, Roger Brown, and Ed Paschke), and recent directions. The museum also has extensive holdings of artists' books. These holdings are comprised largely of handmade and/or artist-produced books usually published in limited editions. Among those represented in the 2,000-volume collection are such seminal pioneers as Dieter Roth, Ed Ruscha, Sol Lewitt, John Cage, Richard Long, and Lucas Samaras, as well as younger innovators like Joan Lyons and Buzz Spector.

The museum's exhibition schedule consists of a balance of twentieth-century historical surveys, investigations of new trends, and examinations of major contemporary artists and ideas. Among the recent showings have been "A Primal Spirit: Ten Contemporary Japanese Sculptors," "Toward the Future: Selections from the Permanent Collection," "Three Decades: The Oliver-Hoffman Collection," "Chicago Artists in the European Tradition," and "Robert Mapplethorpe: The Perfect Moment."

The "Options" series seeks to provide museum audiences with opportunities to view works, often experimental in nature, by new contemporary artists. The museum also develops touring art exhibitions that are shown in venues around the world, including "Abakanowicz," "Gerhard Richter: Paintings," "Christian Boltanski: Lessons of Darkness," and "Gordon Matta-Clark: A Retrospective."

The Museum of Contemporary Art provides an intensive educational program that includes gallery talks and tours, outreach services, lecture series, publications, traveling exhibitions to schools, and an orientation space with videotaped programs to acquaint visitors with current exhibitions.

NEWBERRY LIBRARY

60 West Walton Street
Chicago, Illinois 60610
312/943-9090

Hours Regenstein Reading Room and Reference and Bibliographic Center and Special Collections Reading Room—Tuesday–Thursday, 10–6; Friday–Saturday, 9–5. Exhibition galleries—Monday, Friday, and Saturday, 9–5:30; Tuesday–Thursday, 9–7:30. Public tours— Thursday, 3, and Saturday, 10:30. *Admission* Free.

The Newberry Library is not a museum, but it has invaluable collections that are the basis of numerous exhibitions in two exhibit halls in its historic, renovated Cobb Building.

The internationally recognized research library was founded in 1887 under the will of Walter Loomis Newberry, a pioneer Chicago merchant, banker, and land speculator. The original structure was completed in 1893, and a new 10-story bookstack building was added in 1982.

Newberry Library houses an extensive non-circulating collection of rare books, maps, and manuscripts. Its holdings comprise about 1.4 million volumes, 5 million manuscripts, and 75,000 maps that are valued at more than $300 million. They span Western Europe and the Pan-American civilization from the Middle Ages to the twentieth century, focusing on history and the humanities.

Among the special strengths of the library are sixteenth- and seventeenth-century American history, the Italian Renaissance, history of cartography, American Indian and Western history, early philology, American literature, history of printing, calligraphy, English Renaissance literature, his-

Newberry Library.

tory and theory of music, railroad history, Brazilian and Mexican history, and local and family history and genealogy.

The Newberry, one of only 14 major independent research libraries in the United States, has such treasures in its collections as the early illustrated editions of "The Divine Comedy," a first edition of the King James Bible, account book of the Lewis and Clark expedition, a letter written by Michelangelo, Catlin and Bodmer American Indian drawings, a 1456 Roselli portolan navigation chart, seventeenth-century Aztec illustrated manuscript village books, a first edition of the first American novel, "The Whale," and approximately 500 atlases printed before 1820.

In addition to presenting exhibitions based on its collections, Newberry Library offers adult education seminars on a wide range of topics, a series of "Early Music from The

Newberry Library" concerts (also drawn largely from the collections), and numerous other public events.

The library's research and education programs include fellowships amounting to $350,000 yearly; four centers for scholarly research based on particularly strong collections (the history of the American Indian, family and community history, the Renaissance, and cartography); a seminar that allows undergraduate students of 25 Midwestern colleges to perform research in residence at the Newberry; and the Chicago Metro History Fair, an annual competition for high-school students in local and family history.

ORIENTAL INSTITUTE

University of Chicago
1155 East 58th Street
Chicago, Illinois 60637
312/702-9521

Hours Tuesday–Saturday, 10–4; Wednesday, 10–8:30; Sunday, 12–4. Closed holidays, except when the Culture Bus is running. Open holidays when Culture Bus is operating, 12–4.
Admission Free.

The Oriental Institute of the University of Chicago houses one of the world's major collections of ancient Near Eastern artifacts. A large proportion of the objects on display in its museum were excavated by the institute's own field expeditions to Egypt, Iraq, Turkey, Iran, and Syria-Palestine.

Nearly every significant ancient Near Eastern civilization is represented in the collections, which range from 7000 B.C. to A.D. 1000, at this outstanding educational, research, and cultural facility.

Founded in 1919 by Egyptologist James Henry Breasted, the Oriental Institute is devoted to the study of the origins and development of civilizations in the ancient Near East, and serves as a public resource. The institute maintains a staff of researchers in Chicago, as well as numerous field projects in the Near East.

The institute's field of study extends from the Nile Valley in Egypt, through Palestine and Syria, to the Tigris and Euphrates basins, and includes Persia and parts of the old Ottoman Empire.

Expeditions have excavated important sites such as Megiddo, the Biblical city of Armageddon, and the Persian capital, Persepolis. Since 1924, the institute's Epigraphic Survey of Egypt, headquartered at Chicago House in Luxor, has worked to preserve the historical records inscribed on Egypt's ancient temples.

Oriental Institute.

Sumerian-style statuettes, circa 1900–2600 B.C., *exhibited at the Oriental Institute. (photo by Victor J. Boswell)*

The museum has five galleries—Egyptian, Assyrian, Mesopotamian, Persian, and Syro-Palestinian—as well as a lecture hall. Among the artifacts on view are a huge Assyrian winged bull; a colorful inlaid slab from the Egyptian tomb of Nefermaat and his wife, Atet; a statue of young King Tutankhamen; a massive black limestone head of a bull from Persepolis; and a fragment from the Dead Sea Scrolls. Special exhibitions are presented from time to time.

Free guided tours can be arranged for groups. Film showings and slide programs also are available for a nominal fee. Advance reservations are necessary for groups.

JOHN G. SHEDD AQUARIUM

**1200 South Lake Shore Drive
Chicago, Illinois 60605
312/939-2426**

Hours Daily, 9–6. Closed New Year's Day and Christmas.
Admission Includes aquarium and oceanarium—adults, $7;
children 6–17 and senior citizens, $5; children under 6, free. On
Thursday, the admission is $4 for adults and $3 for children 6–17
and senior citizens.

John G. Shedd Aquarium.

The John G. Shedd Aquarium, the world's largest aquarium, is dedicated to furthering public understanding of humankind's relationship to and dependence upon the aquatic environment and its inhabitants. Each year, about one million people come to see and learn about this fascinating world of underwater creatures in the framework of their natural habitats.

The aquarium, opened in 1930, was a gift of John Graves Shedd, a Chicago businessman. It was a pioneer in its field, seeking to simulate the natural surroundings of both salt and fresh water specimens from every climate, continent, and sea.

The aquarium opened a $43-million addition in 1991—the oceanarium, a 170,000-square-foot facility that features

A feeding in the coral reef.

A diver feeds an eel.

whales, dolphins, sea otters, harbor seals, and penguins. It is the largest indoor marine mammal pavilion in the world and doubles the size of the aquarium.

The major exhibit area houses the Pacific Northwest Coastal Habitats containing beluga whales, false killer whales, Pacific white-sided dolphins, harbor seals, and Alaskan sea otters. It also has a shallow tidal pool. Educational presentations of the natural behaviors of marine mammals are held daily in a 1,000-seat amphitheater with multilevel viewing. A 60,000-gallon penguin habitat is located in the Underwater Gallery. Special exhibit areas also are located in the new oceanarium facility.

More than 6,000 specimens can be seen in the aquarium's six main galleries and the popular "Coral Reef"—a 90,000-

gallon tank (40 feet in diameter and 12 feet deep) that holds an array of 300 Caribbean fish, representing 45 species, with a background of corals, sea fans, sponges, and sea whips.

The 90-foot-long galleries, which radiate from the reef, contain 190 exhibition tanks grouped into 6 separate aquatic systems—tropical, temperate, and cold salt water, and tropical, temperate, and cold fresh water. Among the creatures displayed are the dogfish, octopus, angelfish, arowana, yellow tangs, sturgeon, trout, shark, and crustaceans of all types.

The prime attraction is the "Coral Reef," particularly at feeding time. Every day a diver enters the pool to hand feed the reef community of angelfish, damselfish, barracuda, chubs, grunts, spadefish, triggerfish, groupers, tarpon, porkfish, snappers, moray eels, and other sea life.

The aquarium has an extensive educational program that includes group tours, teacher workshops, courses, teaching materials, and lectures. It also is actively engaged in aquatic research and makes several expeditions annually to collect new specimens.

TERRA MUSEUM OF AMERICAN ART

666 North Michigan Avenue
Chicago, Illinois 60611
312/664-3939

Hours Tuesday, 12–8; Wednesday–Saturday, 10–5; Sunday, 12–5; Closed Monday, New Year's Day, Fourth of July, Thanksgiving, and Christmas.
Admission Adults, $4; senior citizens, $2.50; students, $1; children under 12, free.

The Terra Museum of American Art is dedicated to preserving and cultivating an understanding of American

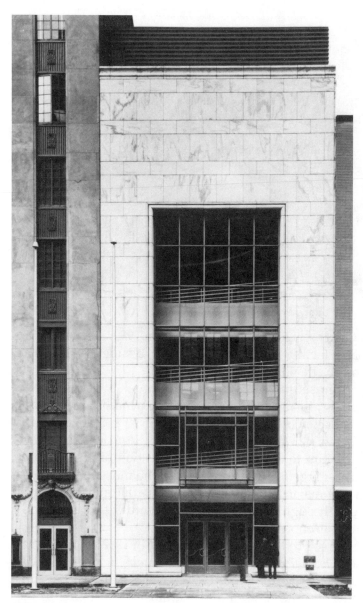

Terra Museum of American Art.

Gallery of the Louvre *by Samuel F. B. Morse.*

Art. Originally founded in Evanston in 1980, it expanded to a major facility on North Michigan Avenue in 1987. The Evanston site now has been closed.

The museum was started by Daniel J. Terra, an industrialist, financier, and entrepreneur who has specialized as a collector of important nineteenth- and twentieth-century American art. In 1981, President Ronald Reagan appointed him to the newly created position of U.S. Ambassador-at-Large for Cultural Affairs. The museum has more than 400 major American works from the mid-nineteenth century through the early twentieth century, and is expanding its collections rapidly.

Terra received widespread coverage in 1982 when he purchased *The Gallery of the Louvre* by Samuel F. B. Morse for $3.2 million. He is a prodigious collector personally and institutionally. He sees himself and the museum bringing to the Midwest "what Whitney brought to New York in the way of

American art." Terra's collection and museum include luminist and other nineteenth-century paintings, American impressionist works, twentieth-century moderns, and works from other periods.

In addition to its permanent collection, the museum offers a wide range of touring and special exhibitions on an ongoing basis. Exhibitions have included "An American Vision: Three Generations of Wyeth Art," "William Merritt Chase: Summers at Shinnecock, 1891–1902," and "Winslow Homer in Gloucester."

The Chicago museum occupies renovated space in two adjoining buildings and eventually will expand into two additional buildings on the same block for a total frontage of 250 feet on North Michigan Avenue.

The museum offers guided tours, gallery talks, lectures, symposia, theater programs, and publications as part of its growing educational program.

III

SPECIALIZED AND LOCAL MUSEUMS AND ORGANIZATIONS

This section is concerned with specialized and local museums and related organizations. It is the largest and most diverse category, having 11 subgroups, dealing with architecture, art, children, ethnicity, history, medicine, the military, natural history, religion, technology, and other fields.

The great bulk of these institutions are local historical societies, with nature centers and ethnic museums following in number. These three types of museums and organizations account for more than two-thirds of the institutions described in the section. Many are located in historic houses, parks, and forest preserves, rather than museum-looking structures.

Visitors to these specialized and local institutions can not only see architectural masterpieces, outstanding works of art, majestic historic houses, and old and new technology, but they can also learn about nature, ethnic customs, medical progress, religious beliefs, and industrial history.

ARCHITECTURAL MUSEUMS AND HOUSES

It was in Chicago that Louis Sullivan, Daniel Burnham, Frank Lloyd Wright, Ludwig Mies van der Rohe, and other architectural giants made their greatest contributions. Examples of their work still can be seen, as well as the designs of such contemporary Chicago architects as Helmut Jahn, Bertrand Goldberg, Harry Weese, and others. Two museum-like organizations—the Chicago Architecture Foundation and the Frank Lloyd Wright Home and Studio Foundation—perpetuate this architectural heritage and by preserving historic buildings, offering architectural tours, and organizing educational programs.

This section also includes the Graham Foundation for Advanced Studies in the Fine Arts, which offers grants, lectures, and exhibitions in the design, architecture, and related fields, and Robie House, considered to be Frank Lloyd Wright's most outstanding creation.

Also see:
Bahá'í House of Worship (Religious Museums)
Historical Pullman Foundation (Historical Museums and Houses)
Numerous historical houses (Historical Museums and Houses)

CHICAGO ARCHITECTURE FOUNDATION

1800 South Prairie Avenue
Chicago, Illinois 60616
312/326-1393

Hours ArchiCenter—Monday–Saturday, 9–6. House tours—April–October: Wednesday, Thursday, and Friday, 12, 1, 2; November–March: Wednesday, Friday, Saturday, and Sunday, 12, 1, 2. Closed Monday, Tuesday, and major holidays. Group tours by appointment.
Admission ArchiCenter, free. House tours—one house, $4; both, $6.

The Chicago Architecture Foundation works to preserve Chicago's architectural heritage and increase public awareness and understanding of the metropolitan area's past, present, and future built environment. It has four principal areas of activity—the ArchiCenter, the Glessner and Clarke Historic Houses, and tours of Chicago's architecture.

The ArchiCenter, located at 330 South Dearborn Street, serves as an architectural information center. It has a museum store on the first floor and exhibition and lecture space on the second level. Changing exhibitions on architecture are presented free to the public.

The John J. Glessner House is architect H. H. Richardson's only surviving design in Chicago. Built in 1886, the structure is known for its bold facade and thoughtful layout around a private courtyard. Original furnishings can be seen in its oak-paneled rooms. Conducted tours also include special exhibitions. The Chicago Architecture Foundation is headquartered in the building.

The Clarke House, Chicago Architecture Foundation.

The Henry B. Clarke House is the oldest surviving house in Chicago. It was built in 1836 in the Greek Revival style and restored by the City of Chicago, which moved it to its present location near the Glessner House. It is furnished by the National Society for the Colonial Dames of America in the State of Illinois, and is open via guided tours.

The foundation offers walking, bus, boat, and bike tours, and over 50 architectural tours of the Loop, neighborhoods, and suburbs, as well as out-of-town trips, are scheduled annually. Well-informed docents provide commentary to enhance the tours.

Graham Foundation. (photo by Richard Nickel)

GRAHAM FOUNDATION FOR ADVANCED STUDIES IN THE FINE ARTS

4 West Burton Street
Chicago, Illinois 60610
312/787-4071

Hours Monday–Thursday, 9–4:30. Closed Friday–Sunday.
Admission Free.

The Graham Foundation is headquartered in the former
Madlener House, a turn-of-the-century landmark mansion,

which is open to the public. The foundation came into existence in 1956 as a result of a bequest from Ernest Robert Graham, Chicago architect and philanthropist. It makes grants in architecture and related arts, including fellowships for advanced study and research, exhibitions, publications, seminars, and other such purposes. The foundation also sponsors free lectures and exhibitions on architecture, design, and related fields.

ROBIE HOUSE

University of Chicago
5757 Woodlawn Avenue
Chicago, Illinois 60637
312/702-8374

Hours Tours—daily, 12.
Admission Adults $3; senior citizens and students, $1.

The Robie House is one of Frank Lloyd Wright's greatest architectural achievements. Built in 1908 for Frederick Robie, the building is a brilliant example of Prairie School architecture and Wright's genius.

The structure's long low lines, the abstract composition of its planes, and cantilevered roof engineering are striking. Exquisite detail, such as the leaded windows of clear and stained glass, the lighting fixtures, and the furnishings, indicate Wright's efforts to relate architecture to peoples' lives.

The Robie House was one of five houses in the Hyde Park/Kenwood neighborhood designed by Wright between 1892 and 1908. Once used as the home for the University of Chicago's Adlai Stevenson Institute of International Affairs, it now serves as the University's Alumni Association Office. Conducted tours are available each noon.

FRANK LLOYD WRIGHT HOME AND STUDIO FOUNDATION

**951 Chicago Avenue
Oak Park, Illinois 60302
708/848-1500**

Hours Monday–Friday, tours at 11, 1, and 3; Saturday–Sunday, 11–4 (continuous tours).
Admission March–October: adults, $5; students under 18 and senior citizens, $3; children under 10, free. November–February: adults, $4; students and senior citizens, $2.

Between 1889 and 1909, Frank Lloyd Wright designed and built more than 125 buildings in his original architectural style known as the Prairie School. Twenty-five of these struc-

Frank Lloyd Wright Home and Studio, West facade, restored to its 1909 design. (photo by Don Kalec)

The children's playroom in the Frank Lloyd Wright Home.

tures still remain in Oak Park, including the noted architect's own home and studio.

It was in Wright's first home and studio in Oak Park that he created his revolutionary design style. He designed the home for his bride in 1889, when he was 22 years of age. It originally was a simple shingle-style cottage with an arched inglenook fireplace, a Dutch-door entrance, and a veranda. As his family grew, Wright began a series of remodelings that added a new kitchen wing, a dining room, a children's playroom, and recessed balconies.

As Wright's architectural practice expanded, he built a studio on the same property as his home in 1898. His love of geometric forms found expression in the art-glass panels of the reception room and in the octagonal library. A two-story-high drafting room, centered around a massive fireplace, held a balcony suspended by chains from the roof beams.

Wright's business and fame spread, but by 1909 he had separated from his wife, closed the studio, and moved from Oak Park. The Oak Park years were his most prolific, producing such architectural masterpieces as the Unity Temple, Larkin Office Building, and the Robie and Coonley Houses.

Designated a National Historic Landmark in 1976, the Wright Home and Studio is located along the tree-lined streets of the Frank Lloyd Wright Prairie School of Architecture National Historic District that contains 25 structures designed by Wright, including his first public building, the Unity Temple.

The Frank Lloyd Wright Home and Studio Foundation was founded in 1974 to acquire and preserve the Wright Home and Studio. The National Trust for Historic Preservation purchased the property and turned it over to the foundation for operation and restoration for the public benefit.

The foundation operates the Oak Park Tour Center, which provides guided tours of the Wright Home and Studio and the Oak Park historic district; offers architectural lectures, exhibitions, excursions, and children's programs; runs a bookstore; and operates the Research Center, which collects historical materials on Wright's architecture and family history.

ART MUSEUMS AND GALLERIES

Once you look beyond the three leading institutions—the Art Institute of Chicago, the Museum of Contemporary Art, and the Terra Museum of American Art—Chicago-area art museums and galleries are found largely on university campuses. They tend to be relatively limited in space and scope, but elegant galleries with excellent collections.

Two such museums can be found at the University of Chicago—the David and Alfred Smart Museum of Art and the Renaissance Society. Other university galleries are the Mary and Leigh Block Gallery at Northwestern University; the Martin D'Arcy Gallery of Art at Loyola University; the Chicago, Ward, and CIU Art Lounge galleries at the University of Illinois at Chicago; the Museum of Contemporary Photography at Columbia College; and galleries at Barat, Lake Forest, and Rosary colleges.

Other institutions in this section are the Lizzadro Museum of Lapidary Art and a number of community art centers. The State of Illinois also has an art gallery at its new building located at 100 West Randolph Street in Chicago. Galleries can be found at many ethnic museums, as indicated below. Although not museums, representative commercial art galleries are listed in the appendices.

Also see:
Art Institute of Chicago (The Big Three)
Balzekas Museum of Lithuanian Culture (Ethnic Museums)

Chicago Public Library Cultural Center (Major Museums and Similar Institutions)
DuSable Museum of African American History (Ethnic Museums)
Mexican Fine Arts Center Museum (Ethnic Museums)
Museum of Contemporary Art (Major Museums and Similar Institutions)
Romanian Folk Art Museum (Ethnic Museums)
Terra Museum of American Art (Major Museums and Similar Institutions)
Ukrainian Institute of Modern Art (Ethnic Museums)

Beverly Art Center. (photo by Elmer Johnson)

BEVERLY ART CENTER

2153 West 111th Street
Chicago, Illinois 60643
312/445-3838

Hours Monday–Friday, 9–5; Saturday, 10–2; Sunday, 1–4. Some evenings.
Admission Free.

Exhibitions, performances, lectures, and an annual art auction in February and arts festival in June are among the offerings at this large arts complex on Chicago's Southwest Side. Two exhibition galleries, a theater, art school, and extensive art collection can be found at this community arts center. Day and evening classes for children and adults in visual and performing arts also are offered.

MARY AND LEIGH BLOCK GALLERY

Northwestern University
1967 Sheridan Road
Evanston, Illinois 60201
708/491-4000

Hours Tuesday–Wednesday, 12–5; Thursday–Sunday, 12–8. Monday by appointment.
Admission Free.

The Mary and Leigh Block Gallery at Northwestern University offers a wide variety of visual art exhibitions that focus on the experimental and the educational. With each changing exhibition, the gallery offers public programs that in-

Mary and Leigh Block Gallery. (photo by James Riggs-Bonamici)

clude lecture series, symposia, performances, guided tours, and daytime lecture programs. Through its extensive programming and commitment to scholarship in the arts, the Block Gallery provides a vital interdisciplinary cultural resource for the regional community.

The Block Gallery's outdoor sculpture garden represents a major center in the Midwest for monumental outdoor sculpture by some of this century's most important modernists, including Joan Miro, Jean Arp, Barbara Hepworth, Henry Moore, and Jacques Lipchitz.

Exhibitions presented at the gallery include "Supreme Instants: The Photography of Edward Weston," "Landscape Drawings of Five Centuries, 1400–1900: From the Robert Lehman Collection," "Brucke: German Expressionist Prints from the Granvil and Marcia Specks Collection," "Wild Spirits, Strong Medicine: African Art and the Wilderness," "A Different War: Vietnam in Art," and "Secessionism and Austrian Graphic Art 1900–1920 from the Collection of the Neue Galerie der Stadt, Linz."

CHICAGO AND A. MONTGOMERY WARD GALLERIES AND CIU ART LOUNGE

University of Illinois at Chicago
Campus Programs
300 Chicago Circle Center (M/C 118)
750 South Halsted Street
Chicago, Illinois 60607

CIU Art Lounge
University of Illinois at Chicago
Chicago Illini Union
828 South Wolcott Street
Chicago, Illinois 60612
312/413-5070

Hours Chicago Gallery—Monday–Friday, 9–5; Ward Gallery—
Monday–Friday, 11–5; CIU Lounge—Monday–Friday, 9–5.
Closed weekends.
Admission Free.

The University of Illinois has three galleries: the Chicago Gallery and the A. Montgomery Ward Gallery in the Chicago Circle Center building on its east Chicago campus and the CIU Art Lounge in the Chicago Illini Union on the west campus.

The Chicago Gallery is part of the student lounge and displays art work of an educational nature, while the Ward Gallery and the CIU Art Lounge are traditional galleries featuring established and faculty artists. Exhibitions normally run four weeks.

COUNTRYSIDE ART CENTER

408 North Vail Avenue
Arlington Heights, Illinois 60004
708/253-3005

Hours Tuesday–Sunday, 1–5. Closed Monday.
Admission Free.

Exhibitions and classes in painting, design, and photography are offered by this community art center.

MARTIN D'ARCY GALLERY OF ART

Loyola University
6525 North Sheridan Road
Chicago, Illinois 60626
312/508-2679

Hours Monday, Wednesday, Friday, 12–4; Tuesday–Thursday, 12–4 and 6–9; Sunday, 1–4. Closed when school is not in session.
Admission Free.

The Martin D'Arcy Gallery of Art is a small but exquisite museum located in a single room in the Elizabeth M. Cudahy Library on the Lake Shore Campus of Loyola University. Featured are approximately 150 objects in its collection, dating from 1100 to 1700. No other Chicago-area museum focuses on the art work of this rich period.

Medieval, Renaissance, and Baroque paintings, sculpture, enamels, textiles, and objects in silver, gold, bronze, and ivory can be seen at the gallery. One of the more spectacular offerings is the sixteenth-century jewel box from Nurem-

Martin D'Arcy Gallery of Art.

berg, which is believed to have come from the collection of Queen Christina of Sweden. Other attractions include the fifteenth-century marble mourning figure from the tomb of the King of Aragon, Fernando de Antequera, and a jeweled and enameled gold sixteenth-century pendant cross from the Crown Jewels of Portugal.

A 10,000-volume library of books on Western art from the twelfth through the eighteenth century is maintained as part of the university's library.

DEERPATH GALLERY

1 Market Square Court
Lake Forest, Illinois 60045
708/234-3743

Hours Monday–Saturday, 10–4. Closed Sunday.
Admission Free.

Exhibitions by 85 artists from the Deerpath Art League's membership are presented each year, with three or four artists being featured monthly. The league also presents a juried art show of 250 artists and craftsmen on Labor Day weekend, as well as year-round classes in weaving, etching, sculpture, and painting.

EVANSTON ART CENTER

2603 Sheridan Road
Evanston, Illinois 60201
708/475-5300
Hours Monday–Saturday, 10–4; Thursday evening, 7–10; Sunday, 2–5. Closed holidays.
Admission Donation.

The Evanston Art Center is both a gallery and a school. The center produces six to eight exhibitions of contemporary art each year, focusing primarily on emerging Midwestern artists, while its studios and classrooms are used to help aspiring artists.

Special exhibitions, lectures, and workshops are presented at the center, including an annual holiday market. It offers more than 150 classes annually in beginning through advanced painting, drawing, fibers, printmaking, silkscreen, photography, ceramics, figure sculpture, jewelry, and metal sculpture, as well as a Youth Fine Arts Program for children of all ages.

HYDE PARK ART CENTER

1701 East 53rd Street
Chicago, Illinois 60615
312/324-5520

Hours Tuesday–Saturday, 11–5. Closed Sunday–Monday.
Admission Free.

Changing exhibitions are presented monthly at this long-established art center in the Hyde Park neighborhood. Art classes, lectures, and other activities also are available.

Lizzadro Museum of Lapidary Art.

Jeweled ivory elephant, Lizzadro Museum.

LIZZADRO MUSEUM OF LAPIDARY ART

220 Cottage Hill Avenue
Elmhurst, Illinois 60126
708/833-1616

Hours Tuesday–Saturday, 10–5; Sunday, 1–5. Closed New
Year's Day, Easter, Fourth of July, Thanksgiving, and Christmas.
Admission Adults, $1; children 12–19, senior citizens, and
students, 50¢; children under 13, teachers, and
school groups, free. Friday, free.

Dedicated exclusively to the beauty of stone carving and the
mysteries of earth science, the Lizzadro Museum is the result
of over 50 years of collecting by the Joseph F. Lizzadro
family. The museum was founded for the public apprecia-
tion of lapidary art and the promotion of the study of earth
science.

The museum houses a famous collection of Chinese jade
and other hard-stone carvings from antique to modern.
Other displays include animal dioramas carved in Germany,
stone intarsias and mosaics from Italy, and mineral
specimens and gemstones from around the world. The
"Rock and Mineral Experience" allows visitors to view such
phenomena as fluorescent rocks, a bending rock, fossils, and
a gold castle, to name a few.

Lectures, demonstrations, and films are held every first
and third Saturday of the month. Group tours can be arranged by appointment. "Gems of the Americas" program is
shown every Sunday at 3 P.M.

MUSEUM OF CONTEMPORARY PHOTOGRAPHY

Columbia College Chicago
600 South Michigan Avenue
Chicago, Illinois 60605
312/663-1600

Hours September–May: Monday–Friday, 10–5; Saturday, 12–5.
Summer: Monday–Friday 10–4; Saturday, 12–4. Closed August,
New Year's Eve, New Year's Day, Martin Luther King's
Birthday, Memorial Day, Fourth of July, Labor Day,
Thanksgiving, Christmas Eve, and Christmas Day.
Admission Free.

Museum of Contemporary Photography. (photo by William Frederking)

Looking down on the East and West Galleries. (photo by William Frederking)

The Museum of Contemporary Photography, formerly known as the Center for Contemporary Photography, was founded by Columbia College Chicago to collect, exhibit, and promote contemporary photography. Since 1976, it has produced more photo exhibitions of this type than any other major institution in the nation, and is the only museum in the Midwest with an exclusive commitment to the medium of photography.

The museum recognizes photography's many roles—as a form of artistic expression, a documenter of human life, a commercial industry, and a tool serving science and technology. Its permanent collection of more than 2,000 photographs and special exhibitions reflects this diversity, covering documentary, industry, fashion, news, science, and other subjects.

It also is possible to view recent works by Midwest photographers in the Print Study Room. In 1982, the museum started The Chicago Photographers Project (now the Midwest Photographers Project), Print Study Room, which enables curators, dealers, critics, and the public to see representative photographs on loan from leading photographers. The works are changed periodically. The Print Study Room houses more than a thousand prints by sixty photographers, with five added annually.

NORTH SHORE ART LEAGUE

620 Lincoln Avenue
Winnetka, Illinois 60093
708/446-2870

Hours Monday–Saturday, 9–10. Closed Sunday.
Admission Free.

The North Shore Art League, which has been in operation since 1924, exhibits the work of its artist members in its gallery. It is best known for its print show in the spring.

The league also organizes crafts, mixed media, and a major craft festival in May and arts festival in September at the Old Orchard shopping center. Classes in such areas as portraiture, contemporary art, photoserigraphy, etching, lithography, jewelry, and creative stitchery are also offered.

SISTER GUALA O'CONNOR ART GALLERY

Rosary College
7900 West Division Street
River Forest, Illinois 60305
708/366-2490
Hours Monday–Friday, 12–4. Closed weekends.
Admission Free.

This Rosary College campus gallery is operated by the art department and shows paintings, sculpture, and other art works from time to time. It is located on the fourth floor with the department.

PARK FOREST ART CENTER

410 Lakewood Boulevard
Park Forest, Illinois 60466
708/748-3377

Hours Monday, Tuesday, Thursday, and Friday, 1–3; Monday and Thursday, 7:30 P.M.–9 P.M.; Saturday, 10–3.
Closed Sunday and Wednesday.
Admission Free.

The Park Forest Art Center has a permanent collection of more than 200 prize-winning works of art displayed in the public library and other public buildings, a rental and sales gallery, and monthly exhibitions.

REICHER GALLERY

Barat College
700 Westleigh Road
Lake Forest, Illinois 60045
708/234-3000

Hours Monday–Saturday, 12–4. Closed Sunday.
Admission Free.

Works of art are shown regularly at this college gallery on the ground level of the main building at Barat College. The gallery has six professional shows covering contemporary art each year, as well as an exhibition of senior student works in May.

RENAISSANCE SOCIETY

University of Chicago
5811 South Ellis Avenue
Chicago, Illinois 60637
312/962-8670

Hours October–June: Tuesday–Friday, 10–4; Saturday–Sunday, 12–4. Closed holidays.
Admission Free.

Founded in 1915, the Renaissance Society is the oldest continuously operating gallery in Chicago devoted exclusively to the temporary exhibition of avant-garde art. It has introduced the Midwest to many important artists.

Located on the university's main quadrangle in a landmark building designed by Henry Ives Cobb, the gallery is a noncollecting museum that emphasizes the investigation of new ideas and methods, rather than serving as a repository for art.

Five temporary exhibitions of avant-garde art are presented each year. Nearly all of the shows are curated by the society's staff. In the 1920s, the gallery exhibited the work of Picasso, Matisse, Rouault, Brancusi, and Lipchitz. One-artist exhibitions by Isamu Noguchi, Fernand Leger, Alexander Calder, and Laszlo Moholy-Nagy were held in the 1930s, as were group showings of Jean Arp, Joan Miro, Paul Klee, Wassily Kandinsky, and Piet Mondrian. In the years that followed, the works of René Magritte, Ludwig Mies van der Rohe, Ben Shahn, and Henry Moore were displayed.

In addition to exhibitions, the society sponsors concerts, performances, film showings, readings, and lectures by noted contemporary artists and critics.

Renaissance Society.

DAVID AND ALFRED SMART MUSEUM OF ART

University of Chicago
5550 South Greenwood Avenue
Chicago, Illinois 60637
312/702-0200

Hours Tuesday–Saturday, 10–4; Sunday, 12–4.
Closed Monday and holidays.
Admission Free.

The David and Alfred Smart Museum of Art serves as the University of Chicago's fine arts museum, offering a permanent collection spanning 4,000 years of art and special

David and Alfred Smart Museum of Art, east entrance.

Inside the Smart Museum.

exhibitions that range over the spectrum of the arts. One of Chicago's most elegant and intimate museums, the gallery is part of the Cochrane-Woods Art Center that also encompasses the university's Department of Art.

The museum's collections are rich in ceramics from ancient Greece; prints and drawings, with particular strength in German Expressionism; the sculpture of such Modern masters as Augusta Rodin, Henri Matisse, Jacques Lipchitz, and Henry Moore; American Regionalist paintings; and furniture and architectural fixtures by Frank Lloyd Wright and other Prairie School designers.

Special exhibitions organized by the gallery staff, as well as traveling exhibitions from other museums, are presented on such diverse topics as Chinese porcelain, abstract paintings by Barnett Newman, Russian painting of the late nineteenth century, the art of black Americans during the civil rights movement, Japanese scrolls of the early-Modern period, the works of Joan Miro, and drawings, prints, and sculpture of Henry Moore. Educational programs such as lectures, symposia, films, and gallery talks are presented frequently in conjunction with exhibitions.

SONNENSCHEIN GALLERY

Lake Forest College
East Deerpath and North Sheridan Roads
Lake Forest, Illinois 60045
708/234-3100

Hours Daily, 2:30–5.
Admission Free.

The Sonnenschein Gallery, located on the top floor of the Henry Durand Art Institute building, schedules temporary exhibitions on a regular basis.

SOUTH SIDE COMMUNITY ART CENTER

3831 South Michigan Avenue
Chicago, Illinois 60653
312/373-1026

Hours Wednesday–Friday, 1–5; Saturday, 9–5.
Closed Sunday–Tuesday.
Admission Free.

This community art center was developed in the 1930s to encourage black artists and writers. It presents changing art exhibitions as well as classes and an annual art auction in May.

STATE OF ILLINOIS ART GALLERY

State of Illinois Building
100 West Randolph Street
Chicago, Illinois 60601
312/917-5322

Hours Monday–Friday, 10–6. Closed weekends.
Admission Free.

This branch of the Illinois State Museum in Springfield is located on the second floor of the new State of Illinois Building in Chicago's Loop. Created in 1985 to exhibit the finest contemporary and historical art produced in the state, it features exhibitions organized by the Illinois State Museum and Illinois Arts Council. The exhibits usually are scheduled for six weeks.

SUBURBAN FINE ARTS CENTER

777 Central Avenue
Highland Park, Illinois 60035
708/432-1888

Hours Monday–Friday, 9:30–4. Closed weekends.
Admission Free.

This community arts center has a gallery that exhibits the works of well-known area artists. Classes for children and adults in sculpture, drawing, painting, and photography also are offered, as well as lectures and workshops on a regular basis.

CHILDREN'S MUSEUMS

The Chicago area has three museums especially for children: The Chicago Children's Museum, Kohl Children's Museum, and Adventures in Wonderland. All have exhibits and programs geared to the scale, interest, and comprehension of youngsters.

A number of large museums also have special exhibits and programs in their fields tailored to children. For example, the Art Institute has an education center with programs for children and families, the Field Museum of Natural History offers the "Place for Wonder," and the Museum of Science and Industry has "The Curiosity Place: an Exhibit for Young Children."

Also see:

Art Institute of Chicago (The Big Three)
**Chicago Academy of Sciences (Major Museums and
    Similar Institutions)**
Field Museum of Natural History (The Big Three)
Museum of Science and Industry (The Big Three)

ADVENTURES IN WONDERLAND

441 South Boulevard
Oak Park, Illinois 60302
708/524-0060

Hours Monday–Friday, 9:30–5 (Wednesday until 8);
Saturday, 12–4. Closed Sunday.
Admission Adults, $2; children $3.50.

Adventures in Wonderland is a children's activity center
and museum in Oak Park. It has changing thematic exhibits,
focusing on such topics as dinosaurs, the circus, and
storybook magic. Aimed at children from toddlers to 9, the
facility enables youngsters to climb aboard a pirate ship,
explore a treehouse, dress up in costumes, and engage in
other such activities.

THE CHICAGO CHILDREN'S MUSEUM

435 East Illinois Street, Suite 370
Chicago, Illinois 60611
312/527-1000

Hours School Year: Tuesday–Friday, 12:30–4:30; Thursday,
12:30–4:30; Saturday–Sunday, 10–4:30. Summer:
Tuesday–Sunday 10–4:30; Thursday, 10–4:30 and 5–8.
Admission Adults, $3; senior citizens, students, and children, $2.

The Chicago Children's Museum (formerly Express-Ways
Children's Museum), was founded on the philosophy that
the arts are vital ingredients in the learning process and that

learning often comes best by doing, rather than through passive viewing.

Initiated by the Junior League of Chicago, the museum first opened in 1982 at a temporary location in the Chicago Public Library Cultural Center. In 1986, it moved to the Lincoln Park Cultural Arts Center, and now is located in North Pier Terminal.

Children have a sensory learning experiences through participatory exhibits, drop-in family sessions, career fairs, traveling exhibitions, and outreach services. Typical exhibits have been "Amazing Chicago," a mini-city of Chicago buildings from 3 to 10 feet high with hidden architectural elements for children to identify and draw, and "Touch Business," designed to stimulate children to explore the sense of touch through a tactile tunnel.

The museum has 16,500 square feet of exhibit space; collections of African arts and crafts and international dolls; and education, van, and school loan programs.

KOHL CHILDREN'S MUSEUM

165 Green Bay Road
Wilmette, Illinois 60091
708/256-6056

Hours Tuesday–Saturday, 10–4; Sunday, 12–4. Closed Monday, Easter, Memorial Day, Fourth of July, Rosh Hashanah, Yom Kippur, Thanksgiving, and Christmas.
Admission Adults and children $2.50; senior citizens, $2.25; children under 1, free.

This hands-on children's museum is an outgrowth of the Kohl Teacher Centers developed by Dolores Kohl Solavy, a former elementary school teacher who established the Dolores Kohl Education Foundation in 1972 to enhance children's learning by supporting exemplary teaching. In addition to the Wilmette education center, the foundation operates two facilities in Israel and has helped spawn similar centers worldwide.

The Kohl Children's Museum opened in 1985. It is designed for children to use all their senses in understanding concepts and the world around them. The participatory exhibits deal with areas such as music, colors, literature, bubbles, telecommunications, newspapers, supermarkets, educational toys, and the ancient world of Jerusalem.

It also has a Discovery Center, an educational learning environment where parents and children are involved in creating art, games, and educational projects. It includes a Design Lab, which allows children to create their own educational materials, with machines and models as inspiration. Twelve learning stations were installed in 1990, dealing with such subjects as art, bookmaking, geography, and language.

Girls check out the mini Jewel/Osco grocery store exhibit at the Kohl Children's Museum.

ETHNIC MUSEUMS

Chicago is a city of ethnic diversity and many of these ethnic groups have museums concerned with their history, culture, traditions, arts, and contributions. Fourteen ethnic museums can be found in the metropolitan area.

Two of the largest of these ethnic museums are the Du-Sable Museum of African American History and the Bal-zekas Museum of Lithuanian Culture. The Jews, Poles, Swedes, and Ukrainians have two such museums. One institution, the National Italian American Sports Hall of Fame, is restricted to a single field. Another, the Mitchell Indian Museum, is a collection of artifacts on a college campus.

Also see:
Morton B. Weiss Museum of Judaica (Religious Museum)

Stained glass at the Balzekas Museum of Lithuanian Culture. (photo by
Jonas Tamulaitis)

BALZEKAS MUSEUM OF LITHUANIAN CULTURE

6500 South Pulaski Road
Chicago, Illinois 60629
312/847-1515

Hours Daily, 10–4. Closed New Year's Day and Christmas.
Admission Adults, $3; senior citizens and students, $2; children,
$1.

The Balzekas Museum of Lithuanian Culture is dedicated to
the preservation and perpetuation of Lithuanian art, history,
customs, and traditions in the free world. It offers a comprehensive collection of antiquities, art, artifacts, literature,
and memorabilia spanning 1,000 years of Lithuanian culture, including a Children's Museum of Immigrant History,

which serves as a cultural and educational resource for children, families, schools, and the public.

Upgraded and expanded exhibits have come with the renovated three-story former hospital facilities that the museum now occupies. The principal new exhibit—"Lithuania Through the Ages"—contains artifacts, medieval arms and armor, and rare prints, maps, books, coins, paintings, and other materials from when Lithuania was independent. Other initial exhibits deal with outstanding Lithuanian women, the sights and crafts of Lithuania, the commercial photography of Kantytis Izokaitis, and some 100 works by 20 artists of Lithuanian background.

The new children's section and workshop offers educational programs to young people and their parents, and the museum's reputation as a Lithuanian research and resource center has been enhanced by the addition of a 45,000-volume library. The museum also has expanded its program of folkart skills and includes instruction in Easter egg coloring, ornament design, basketweaving, textiles, and weaving.

The Balzekas Museum's collection of armor, antique weapons, and rare maps, circa 1550. (photo by Jonas Tamulaitis)

COPERNICUS CULTURAL AND CIVIC CENTER

5216 West Lawrence Avenue
Chicago, Illinois 60630
312/777-8898
Hours Vary with special events.
Admission Depends upon event.

This Polish cultural center, opened in 1981, also serves as a civic center for the Northwest section of Chicago. It displays artifacts, books, paintings, and tapestries, and has a 2,000-seat theater offering vintage films and live shows. In addition, special events and temporary exhibits are presented from time to time.

CZECHOSLOVAK HERITAGE MUSEUM, LIBRARY, AND ARCHIVES

2701 South Harlem Avenue
Berwyn, Illinois 60402
708/795-5800

Hours Monday–Friday, 10–4. Closed weekends.
Admission Donation.

The Czechoslovak Heritage Museum, Library, and Archives, founded in 1974, is operated by CSA Fraternal Life, which was known as the Czechoslovak Society of America until 1982. Located in Berwyn, it seeks to preserve and promote Czechoslovak culture, history, and art.

The museum contains a colorful collection of folk costumes from many different villages and regions; dolls that depict the dress of still other areas; paintings and sculptures by artists of many eras; fine blown glass and lead crystal in many colors and styles; hundreds of handmade Easter eggs decorated through a variety of techniques; and many examples of china, ceramics, leather goods, embroidery, farm implements, and musical instruments.

Periodic displays usually feature historic events, prominent figures of America and Czechoslovakia, and seasonal customs and traditions.

DuSABLE MUSEUM OF AFRICAN AMERICAN HISTORY

740 East 56th Place
Chicago, Illinois 60637
312/947-0600

Hours Monday–Friday, 9–5; Saturday–Sunday, 12–5. Closed New Year's Day, Easter, and Christmas.
Admission Adults, $1; children and students, 50¢. Thursday, free.

The DuSable Museum of African American History has evolved from a family project in 1961 into one of the nation's most outstanding museums dedicated to African-American history and culture. This ethnic museum was started by Margaret and Charles Burroughs in their home because they believed the public should have a better understanding of black history, art, culture, and contributions to the nation and world. It was named for Jean Batiste Pointe DuSable, a black Haitian trader who was the first settler in Chicago.

Today, the DuSable Museum occupies a renovated and expanded facility in Washington Park. It has become the center of a wide range of cultural activities celebrating the achievements of black Americans, including exhibits, lec-

DuSable Museum of African-American History.

tures, films, classes, teacher workshops, publications, book fairs, and community events.

Among the permanent exhibits are 56 paintings depicting "Blacks in Early Illinois"; a series of murals by Eugene Eda showing persons who have made significant contributions to black American history; and collections of sculpture, masks, drums, dolls, jewelry, textiles, musical instruments, and other objects from Africa. Traveling and locally developed temporary exhibitions are presented from time to time on topics relating to African-American history and culture.

The DuSable Museum also has an extensive library and publications program. In addition to thousands of volumes, the library contains an extensive file of biographical, topical, and social activist material such as posters, handbills, letters, and documents, as well as photographs, slides, and tapes relating to the black experience.

MEXICAN FINE ARTS CENTER MUSEUM

1852 West 19th Street
Chicago, Illinois 60608
312/738-1503

Hours Tuesday–Sunday, 10–5. Closed Monday.
Admission Free.

The Mexican Fine Arts Center Museum is the first Mexican museum in the Midwest and the largest of its kind in the nation. Its mission is to showcase the richness and beauty of Mexican culture in all of its manifestations.

The museum is the only facility of its kind in the nation that can hold both large visual art exhibits as well as performing arts events. The museum has three galleries and its major exhibits change every three months. Exhibits range from the very traditional to the avant-garde.

The museum is host to over 600 school groups a year and tours are available in Spanish or English for groups. Two weeks notice is required.

The museum annually presents the largest Day of the Dead exhibit held in the nation. It also offers productions in dance, theater, music, and poetry.

Western Apache Olla Basket, circa 1890, and headdress from the Mitchell Indian Museum.

MITCHELL INDIAN MUSEUM

Kendall College
2408 Orrington Avenue
Evanston, Illinois 60201
708/866-1395

Hours Monday–Friday, 9–4; Sunday, 1–4. Closed Saturday and in August and on Kendall College holidays.
Admission Free, but donations suggested.

The Mitchell Indian Museum at Kendall College in Evanston was opened in 1977 to house the Indian art and artifact collection of John and Betty Mitchell, who gathered the objects over a half century. The museum now contains gifts from other donors, as well as the Mitchell collection.

Continuing acquisitions have developed the collection's strengths in beadwork, quiltwork, clothing, jewelry, rugs, basketry, pottery, and dolls. Contemporary as well as traditional works are featured in a gallery of permanent exhibits introducing native cultures of the Southwest (primarily Navajo and Pueblo), the Plains, and the Great Lakes regions. In each area display there is a painted scene illustrating everyday life in that region, and a "touching table" with objects to be directly experienced with the senses of touch, hearing, smell, and sight. Another room is used for exhibits that change through the year. Past exhibit subjects have included Pueblo pottery, Navajo textiles, contemporary painting and sculpture by Native American artists, arts of the Northwest Coast cultures, and Native American dolls. Lectures by nationally known scholars and demonstrations by Native American artists are coordinated with these exhibits.

In the hallway between the two exhibit rooms is a small exhibit on "The Ancient Peoples of Illinois."

NATIONAL ITALIAN AMERICAN SPORTS HALL OF FAME

2625 South Clearbrook Drive
Arlington Heights, Illinois 60635
708/437-3077

Hours Monday–Friday, 8:30–4:30. Closed weekends and holidays.
Admission Free.

Outstanding athletes of Italian-American ancestry are honored at this hall of fame, founded in 1977. Seventy-nine sports personalities have been inducted into the hall, includ-

Uniforms exhibit at the National Italian American Sports Hall of Fame.

ing such notables as Rocky Marciano, Joe DiMaggio, Eddie Arcaro, Vince Lombardi, Willie Mosconi, Phil Esposito, Hank Luisetti, Donna Caponi, and Andy Varipapa. The hall of fame purchased the building housing the International Sport Fishing Museum (which moved from the area) in Arlington Heights in 1986, and moved in the following year. It formerly was located in Elmwood Park.

POLISH MUSEUM OF AMERICA

984 North Milwaukee Avenue
Chicago, Illinois 60622
312/384-3352

Hours Daily, 12–5.
Admission Free.

The Polish Museum of America is one of the oldest and largest ethnic museums in the nation. It promotes knowledge of Polish history and culture, especially Polish and Polish-American art in its paintings, sculptures, drawings, and lithographs by well-known artists.

The collections include more than 350 paintings by Polish artists, costumes, religious artifacts, folk art, military uniforms and equipment, and memorabilia of Thaddeus Kosciusko, noted Polish patriot, and Ignace Jan Paderewski, renowned Polish pianist and statesman, who is shown in a special room with his piano.

Among the other highlights are a beautiful 13-by-27-foot stained glass window, titled *Poland Reborn,* which originally was designed in Krakow for the Polish pavilion at the 1939 New York World's Fair; a cast from the central door of the twelfth-century Cathedral of Gniezno that depicts the life of St. Adalbert; and a rotunda shrine commissioned by Polish war veterans for the New York fair.

A 60,000-volume library of publications pertaining to Poland, as well as slides, filmstrips, maps, and photographs, also can be found at the museum. In addition, the museum offers lectures, concerts, motion pictures, slide presentations, and theater performances.

Items on display at the Romanian Folk Art Museum.

ROMANIAN FOLK ART MUSEUM

2526 Ridgeway
Evanston, Illinois 60201
708/328-9099

Hours Saturday, 2–5. Closed Sunday–Friday and holidays.
Admission Donation.

The nation's largest collection of Romanian folk art—as well as the Chicago area's most extensive European folk art collection—is displayed at this Evanston museum. Among the 600 colorful pieces are costumes, rugs, bedspreads, pillow cases, towels, pottery, icons, and painted furniture gathered by Rodica and Michael Perciali, the museum's founders.

Highlights of the museum, which is located in the Perciali home, include 40 costumes from 18 regions of Romania; painted pottery and furniture; 11 beautiful icons on glass showing Byzantine religious subjects; the works of contemporary Romanian artists; and other materials spanning several centuries.

The museum serves as a resource center on Romania and Romanian immigration. It also presents slide shows and outreach exhibitions, has a 500-volume library on Romanian folk art, and sells Romanian arts and crafts.

SPERTUS MUSEUM OF JUDAICA

618 South Michigan Avenue
Chicago, Illinois 60605
312/922-9012

Hours Sunday–Thursday, 10–5; Friday, 10–3; ARTiFACT Center—Sunday–Thursday, 1:30–4:30.
Admission Adults, $3.50; children, senior citizens, and students, $2. Friday, free.

This comprehensive Jewish museum houses nearly 3,000 works spanning 3,500 years of Jewish history and culture. The permanent collection includes ceremonial objects, textiles, jewelry, coins, costumes, artifacts, paintings, sculpture, and graphics. The Zell Holocaust Memorial, as well as regular special exhibits, are important components of the museum.

The Paul and Gabriella Rosenbaum ARTiFACT CENTER is a unique hands-on exhibition that enables children and their families to become archaeologists exploring the ancient Near East. Main features of the exhibit include a 32-foot dig site for unearthing real artifacts, an open marketplace with five special activity stations, a theater/costume area with TV monitor, an illustrated time line, an Israelite House where preschoolers can shake hands with the past, and "Sundays at Two," workshops for children 7 and older.

The Bezalel Ark, a Torah ark made in Israel between 1913 and 1923, exhibited at the Spertus Museum of Judaica.

SWEDISH AMERICAN HISTORICAL SOCIETY

5125 North Spaulding Avenue
Chicago, Illinois 60625
312/583-5722

Hours Monday–Friday by appointment, 8:30–4:30. Closed weekends and holidays.
Admission Free.

The historical society has a program of exhibits, research, archives, meetings, conferences, and publications that deals with the Swedish-American experience. It functions more as a cultural and research center than as a museum.

SWEDISH AMERICAN MUSEUM

5211 North Clark Street
Chicago, Illinois 60640
312/728-8111

Hours Tuesday–Friday, 11–4; Saturday–Sunday 11–3. Closed Monday.
Admission Adults, $1 donation; children, 50¢ donation.

The Swedish American Museum moved to its present location in Andersonville on Chicago's Far North Side in 1988 with the King and Queen of Sweden officiating at the dedication. The permanent exhibit tells the story of the Swedes who built Chicago. Temporary exhibits of famous Swedish men and women or of contemporary Swedish art change every two months.

The museum center offers classes in Swedish language, crafts, and genealogy. Every Swedish holiday is celebrated. A large museum store has everything Swedish from a dalahorse to a Viking helmet.

UKRAINIAN INSTITUTE OF MODERN ART

2320 West Chicago Avenue
Chicago, Illinois 60622
312/227-5522

Hours Tuesday–Sunday, 12–4.
Admission Donation.

The Ukrainian Institute of Modern Art is a cultural art center that presents art exhibitions, contemporary music concerts, dance workshops, lectures, poetry readings, and other such activities in Chicago's Ukrainian neighborhood.

The key ingredient is artwork. The institute has an expanding permanent collection of art work by artists of Ukrainian descent. A year-round schedule of changing exhibitions features contemporary art by artists of non-Ukrainian and Ukrainian descent.

UKRAINIAN NATIONAL MUSEUM

2453 West Chicago Avenue
Chicago, Illinois 60622
312/276-6565

Hours Tuesday–Sunday, 11–4. Closed Monday.
Admission Donation.

Bottle and cups, Ukranian National Museum.

The Ukrainian National Museum consists of three parts: a museum, an archive, and a library. The museum is known for its collection of Ukrainian folk art, but also has many other diverse holdings.

The folk art includes embroideries, wood carvings, ceramics, metal carvings, Easter eggs, dolls, and costumes. The museum also has Ukrainian folk instruments, household items, agricultural implements, and architectural samples.

In addition, numerous paintings, sculpture, and bas-reliefs of modern Ukrainian artists; portraits of prominent Ukrainians; military uniforms, medals, and insignias; and photographs, documents, newspapers, tape recordings, and memorabilia are on display.

The library contains more than 18,000 book titles and a large collection of Ukrainian periodicals, calendars, and almanacs. Posters, pamphlets, manuscripts, and other materials can be found in the archive.

HISTORICAL MUSEUMS AND HOUSES

Historical museums and houses are the most numerous types of museums in the Chicago area and the nation. Almost every sizable community has a historical society for the collection, study, and interpretation of the area's artifacts and memorabilia and the preservation of historical structures. The largest and most prominent historical museum in the region is the Chicago Historical Society, which is described in the Major Museums and Similar Institutions section. This section includes 50 historical museums and houses, ranging from historic log cabins to comprehensive outdoor villages.

Among the diverse historical sights are the Blackberry Historical Farm-Village, Evanston Historical Society, Grosse Point Lighthouse, Highland Park Historical Society, Historic Pullman Foundation, Jane Addams' Hull-House Museum, Illinois and Michigan Canal Museum, Naper Settlement Museum Village, Graue Mill and Museum, Stacy's Tavern, and Seven Acres Antique Village and Museum.

Also see:

Cantigny (Major Museums and Similar Institutions)
Chicago Architecture Foundation (Architectural Museums and Houses)
Chicago Historical Society (Major Museums and Similar Institutions)
Fort Sheridan Museum (Military Museums)
Grand Army of the Republic Memorial and Veteran's Military Museum (Military Museums)

The Grove (Natural History Museums, Conservatories, and Nature Centers)

International Museum of Surgical Sciences (Medical and Health Museums)

Newberry Library (Major Museums and Similar Institutions)

Wood Library-Museum of Anesthesiology (Medical and Health Museums)

Frank Lloyd Wright Home and Studio Foundation (Architectural Museums and Houses)

Jane Addams' Hull-House.

Inside Hull-House.

JANE ADDAMS' HULL-HOUSE MUSEUM

University of Illinois at Chicago
600 South Halsted Street
Chicago, Illinois 60607
312/413-5353
Mailing Address: PO Box 4348, University of Illinois,
Chicago, Illinois 60680.

Hours Summer: Monday–Friday, 10–4; Sunday, 12–5. Winter:
Monday–Friday, 10–4. Closed holidays.
Admission Free.

Hull-House, founded by Jane Addams and Ellen Gates Starr
in 1889, was the first settlement house in Chicago and a
prototype for most that followed. Two of its original build-

ings have been restored by the University of Illinois at Chicago and now are operated as a museum and historic site.

The two buildings, the Hull Mansion (1856) and the Resident's Dining Hall (1905), contain restored rooms and exhibits of artifacts, memorabilia, furniture, paintings, photographs, documents, books, and other materials relating to the life and work of Jane Addams, her associates, and the history of Hull-House.

A major exhibit on the history of the Hull-House neighborhood, located in the Residents' Dining Hall, focuses on the settlement of ethnic groups in the area. A series of slide programs on topics relating to the history of Hull-House and its neighborhood also is offered.

ARLINGTON HEIGHTS HISTORICAL MUSEUM

110 West Fremont
Arlington Heights, Illinois 60004
708/255-1225

Hours Saturday 1–4. Sunday, 2–5. Other times by appointment. Closed holidays.
Admission Adults, $1; children 7–14, 50¢. Special group rates for tours.

Permanent and temporary exhibits, an 1836 log cabin, lectures, films, education programs for children, and a country store are among the offerings of this local historical society, housed in five nineteenth-century buildings.

AURORA HISTORICAL MUSEUM

305 Cedar Street
Aurora, Illinois 60506
708/897-9029

Hours February–December 24: Wednesday, Saturday, and
Sunday, 1–5. Other times by appointment. Carriage
House—May–October: Saturday–Sunday, 1–5. Closed Easter.
Admission Adults, $2, children and senior citizens, $1.

This local history museum, housed in an 1857 mansion with
an 1840 carriage house, contains pioneer and Indian artifacts, 10,000-year-old mastodon bones, Victorian furnishings, timepieces, musical instruments, vehicles, railroad
items, photographs, and nineteenth- and early twentieth-
century tools and household materials. An adjacent carriage
house is devoted to early modes of transportation.

BARRINGTON AREA HISTORICAL MUSEUM CENTER

212-218 West Main Street
Barrington, Illinois 60010
708/381-1730

Hours Thursday–Friday, 10–4; Saturday, 10–1. Closed
Sunday–Wednesday.
Admission Free, but donation suggested.

This museum has been relocated to two restored Victorian
houses and a reconstructed historic barn. The Applebee
House, at 212 West Main Street, contains six period rooms

that interpret the life-style of three families (the Applebees, Wisemans, and Holtzees) that lived in the house between 1889 and 1925. The museum gift shop is located in the adjacent Donlea/Kincaid House (at 218 West Main Street), which is also open on Tuesday and Wednesday.

BATAVIA DEPOT MUSEUM

155 Houston
Batavia, Illinois 60510
708/879-1800

Hours Monday, Wednesday, Friday, Saturday, and Sunday, 2–4.
Closed Tuesday and Thursday.
Admission Free.

The 1854 Batavia Depot, one of the oldest railroad stations on the Burlington Line, is the site of this local history museum containing clothing, tools, railroad equipment, windmills, pioneer materials, genealogical information, historic house photographs, manuscripts, and a Mary Todd Lincoln display.

BLACKBERRY HISTORICAL FARM-VILLAGE

Barnes Road and Galena Blvd.
Aurora, Illinois 60506
708/892-1550

Hours May–Labor Day: daily, 10–4:30. Labor Day–October: Friday–Sunday, 10–4:30.
Admission Nonresidents: adults, $5.50; children, $4.

The rural life of the Midwest in the nineteenth and early twentieth centuries is the theme of this 60-acre living history farm-village. Visitors experience the past by seeing artifacts and demonstrations of rural life-style. Among the attractions of this outdoor museum are 11 Victorian stores, 40 restored carriages and sleighs, a train depot with railroad artifacts, a one-room schoolhouse, a Victorian household with authentic furnishings, a barn and historic farm equipment, an 1840s pioneer cabin, a small train, a carousel, and living exhibits featuring guides in period dress showing how the pioneers lived through spinning, weaving, candle-making, woodworking, pottery-making, farming, and blacksmithing demonstrations. Handmade products are offered for sale.

Many special events are held during the year, such as a Spring Craft and Garden Day in May, Antique Band Organ Rally, and Blacksmithing Weekend in July, Antique Auto Show in August, Indian Summer Day in September, Halloween Ghost Walk in October, and Yuletide Celebration in December.

Demonstrations at Blackberry Historical Farm-Village.

ANDREW C. COOK HOUSE AND MUSEUM

711 North Main Street
Wanconda, Illinois 60084
708/526-9303
Mailing Address: PO Box 256, Wanconda, Illinois 60084.

Hours May–September: Sunday, 1–4; other times by appointment.
Admission Free, but donations accepted.

Housed in an 1840 brick farmhouse built by Lake County pioneer Andrew C. Cook, the museum contains quilts, toys, furniture of the period, artifacts from Wanconda Township, a working loom, and Cook family genealogy. It is operated by the Wanconda Township Historical Society.

DES PLAINES HISTORICAL MUSEUM

789 Pearson Street
Des Plaines, Illinois 60016
708/391-5399

Hours Monday–Friday, 9–4; Sunday, 1–4 (except January, July, and August). Other times and tours by appointment. Closed holidays.
Admission Free.

The 1906 residence of Benjamin F. Kinder, Sr., an early local businessman, serves as a museum for this society concerned with the history of Des Plaines and Maine Township. The building's period rooms depict the 1900–10 life-style, while

Kinder Home, circa 1912, the Des Plaines Historical Museum.

the museum's galleries are devoted to changing historical exhibits. The historical library contains extensive photo, document, map, and microfilm files. The museum is operated by the Des Plaines Historical Society.

STEPHEN A. DOUGLAS TOMB

636 East 35th Street
Chicago, Illinois 60616
312/225-2620

Hours Daily, 9–5.
Admission Free.

The tomb of Stephen A. Douglas, prominent Illinois senator and opponent of Abraham Lincoln for both the senate and the presidency, is located on the property where he lived in Chicago. The site is administered by the Illinois Historic Site Agency.

DOWNERS GROVE HISTORICAL MUSEUM

831 Maple Avenue
Downers Grove, Illinois 60515
708/963-1309

Hours Wednesday, 1–4; Sunday 2–4. Closed all other days and on holidays.
Admission Free.

The Downers Grove Historical Museum—operated jointly by the Downers Grove Park District and the Downers Grove Historical Society—occupies two buildings on property originally owned by Israel and Avis Dodge Blodgett, who settled in the area in 1835.

One building was constructed in 1892 by the Blodgetts' youngest son, Charles. It has Victorian rooms with special exhibits of clothing, crafts, toys, photographs, musical instruments, and other items of the period.

The second building, which has a 1900s barn exterior, actually was erected in 1987. The exhibits here present the farming heritage of the community and the history of the fire department, which was established in 1898. Among the artifacts on display is a 1920 pumper, the fire department's first mechanized equipment.

Plans are under way for an exhibit on early transportation, featuring a plank from the Southwestern Plank Road built in 1851.

DUNDEE TOWNSHIP HISTORICAL SOCIETY

426 Highland Avenue
Dundee, Illinois 60118
708/428-6996

Hours Wednesday and Sunday, 2–4. Other times by appointment.
Admission Free, but donations accepted.

Historical objects from Dundee Township in Kane County can be found in this local museum housed in the original St. Catherine of Sienna school building, built in 1925. Among the features are Indian artifacts, period clothing, histories of township people and places, and Dupre and Allan Pinkerton historic collections.

DUNHAM-HUNT MUSEUM

304 Cedar Avenue St.
Charles, Illinois 60174
708/584-7001

Hours Mid-July–mid-August: daily 1–4; mid-August–mid-June: Wednesday–Sunday, 1–4. Closed holidays.
Admission Free except for tours by appointment, $1.

Built in 1840 by early settler Bela T. Hunt, the Dunham-Hunt House is furnished in grand style with items from the Dunham Castle, built in 1883 by the famed importer of horses Mark W. Dunham. An 1840 room is furnished with items from the Ward family and the American Revolution,

Dunham-Hunt Museum.

including a copy of a Washington letter and a Revere teaspoon. Other rooms contain vintage clothing, children's toys, a library with old books on local history, and original oil paintings by Rosa Bonheur, H. H. Cross, and others. A temporary exhibition room changes exhibits monthly.

DuPAGE COUNTY HISTORICAL MUSEUM

102 East Wesley Street
Wheaton, Illinois 60187
708/682-7343

Hours Monday, Wednesday, Friday, and Saturday, 10–4. Closed Sunday, Tuesday, Thursday, and holidays.
Admission Free.

Located in a 1891 National Register building, the DuPage County Historical Museum features an exhibit that highlights over 150 years (1831–1989) of county history, a Costume Gallery with changing exhibits from the collection, and a Collections Gallery with changing exhibit themes. Period exhibits include a log cabin, general store, Victorian sitting room, and extensive model railroad display. Library, archives, and collections are open for research use. Family, adult, and children's programs are scheduled throughout the year.

DURANT-PETERSON HOUSE

LeRoy Oakes Forest Preserve
Dean Street near Randall Road
St. Charles, Illinois 60174
708/377-6424

Hours June 15–October 15: Sunday, 1–4. Special tours by appointment.
Admission Free.

This is a "house museum" depicting rural life in the Midwest in the 1840s. Costumed guides take visitors on tours of the 1843 prairie house, restored by Restorations of Kane County, with authentic furnishings and hanging herbs and onions from the period. The house is located in LeRoy Oakes Forest Preserve, a half mile west of St. Charles.

ELLWOOD HOUSE MUSEUM

509 North First Street
DeKalb, Illinois 60115
815/756-4609

Hours April 1–first week in December, with guided tours:
Tuesday–Friday, 1 and 3; Saturday–Sunday, 1, 2, and 3. Larger
groups (12 or more) may reserve tours for mornings as well.
Admission Adults, $3.50; children under 12 as part of family
group, free. Group tours by reservation, $2.50 per person;
elementary school groups, $1 per person.

Built in 1879, this 33-room mansion sits on eight stately acres
in DeKalb. The house was occupied by descendants of

Ellwood House Museum. (photo by Jay Elliot)

Nineteenth-century canopy beds grace the Green Bedroom. (photo by Roger Legel)

barbed-wire baron Isaac L. Ellwood until 1964. Guided tours of the opulent home provide insights into how tastes changed in architecture, fashion, and family life from the 1880s to the 1910s. On the grounds are the "Little House"—a Victorian-era playhouse—and the "Carriage House," with exhibits of horse-drawn transportation, early agriculture, and barbed wire. There also is a wildflower study area.

ELMHURST HISTORICAL MUSEUM

120 East Park Avenue
Elmhurst, Illinois 60126
708/833-1457

Hours Tuesday–Sunday, 1–5. Others hours by appointment.
Admission Free.

A massive limestone mansion built in 1892 for Village President Henry Glos and his wife, Lucy, houses Elmhurst's municipal museum. A grant from the National Endowment for the Humanities funded renovation and installation of new interpretive exhibits. Orientation and permanent galleries show the history of the building and the suburb's 150 years of development. Special exhibits and photographic galleries, an auditorium, and a local history research room

Elmhurst Historical Museum. (photo by C. Bruce)

complete the museum's 6,000 square feet of public space. Located in the center of Elmhurst, the museum overlooks scenic Glos Memorial Park.

Evanston Historical Society. (photo by EPS Studios, Inc.)

EVANSTON HISTORICAL SOCIETY AND CHARLES GATES DAWES HOUSE

225 Greenwood Street
Evanston, Illinois 60201
708/475-3410

Hours Monday, Tuesday, Thursday, Friday, and Saturday, 1–5. Closed Sunday, Wednesday, and holidays.
Admission Adults, $3; senior citizens and students, $1.

The Evanston Historical Society is the second largest local historical organization in Illinois. It is headquartered in the former home of Gen. Charles G. Dawes, the nation's vice president in 1925–29. The 28-room mansion, which contains original furnishings from the 1920s, was built in 1894 for Robert D. Sheppard and designed by Henry Edwards-Fichen. It became the home of General Dawes in 1909 and was designated a National Historic Landmark in 1976.

The society maintains sections of the building as a house museum and devotes other areas to exhibitions exploring aspects of Evanston's history. In recent years, the Dawes House library, dining room, and great hall have been restored to their 1925–29 appearance. Among the collections are Dawes memorabilia, local artifacts, costumes, archival material, photographs, and newspapers of the past.

The society also has a 2,500-volume library and reading room, offers lectures and tours, and issues a variety of publications.

GARFIELD FARM MUSEUM

3N016 Garfield Road near Route 38
PO Box 403
LaFox, Illinois 60147
708/584-8485

Hours June–September: Wednesday and Sunday, 1–4.
Tours year-round by appointment.
Admission Adults, $2 donation; children 6–11, $1.

This National Registry of Historic Places site is being developed by volunteers as an 1840s working farm. It contains an 1846 inn, an 1849 barn, and historic poultry equipment. Hourly tours are given at 1–4 P.M. on Wednesday and Sunday in June–September and by appointment year-round.

The Garfield Inn, circa 1846, was once a teamster and stagecoach shop.

The farm is located in Campton Township on Route 38 (Roosevelt Road), about 40 miles west of Geneva.

GENEVA HISTORICAL SOCIETY MUSEUM

Wheeler Park Highway 31
Geneva, Illinois 60134
708/232-4951

Hours April–December: Wednesday, Saturday, and Sunday, 2–4:30.
Admission Donation.

The Geneva Historical Society Museum has four large exhibit rooms filled with collections and exhibits from pioneer days to the early twentieth century. The largest collections consist of mid-nineteenth-century furniture, silver, china, and paintings. Among the other offerings are exhibits dealing with jewelry, toys, household articles, and industrial

Geneva Historical Society Museum.

tools. The resource center contains Illinois County histories, reference books, atlases, local directories, family folders, a microfilm reader for census and newspaper collections, and a tape-slide machine of local programs.

GLENVIEW AREA HISTORICAL SOCIETY

1121 Waukegan Road
Glenview, Illinois 60025
708/724-2235

Hours Sunday, 1–4; other times by appointment.
Admission Free.

The Glenview Area Historical Society, founded in 1964, is housed in an 1864 farmhouse. It has an extensive collection of period furniture and art objects, as well as a clothing collection and memorabilia of early area residents.

An archival library is located in its own coach house on the society grounds, completed in 1981. It contains records of the area and is available for research.

Inside Graue Mill.

GRAUE MILL AND MUSEUM

York and Spring Roads
Oak Brook, Illinois 60521
708/655-2090

Hours mid-April–mid-November: daily, 10–5.
Admission Adults, $1.50, children 3–15 and senior citizens, 50¢; children under 3, free.

In 1852, Fred Graue turned the wheel to open the sluice gates of the Graue Mill. Water flowed from Salt Creek and the huge wooden waterwheel began to turn. As grain was fed into the hopper above the spinning buhrstones, golden cornmeal streamed into the box below. This same process can be seen today at the Graue Mill and Museum—the only operating waterwheel gristmill in Illinois. A white-aproned miller/guide explains the milling process.

Graue Mill is also one of the few authentic Underground Railway stations in Illinois, and Civil War relics can be seen on the ground floor. The upper two floors that served as the granary have been converted to exhibits and feature a collection of historical objects from the 1840–85 period. The second floor looks and feels like an old-fashioned barn, with hay, a two- seated sleigh, farm implements, and other such items. The top floor has been divided into four rooms—a child's room, a Victorian drawing room, a kitchen with a sitting room, and an old country store.

Weavers and spinners demonstrate daily and handwoven items may be purchased as well as cornmeal and whole-wheat flour.

GROSSE POINT LIGHTHOUSE

2601 Sheridan Road
Evanston, Illinois 60201
708/328-6961

Hours June–September: weekends or by appointment.
Admission Adults, $1.50; children, 75¢.

The Grosse Point Lighthouse was built by the federal government in 1873 as the lead lighthouse marking the approach to Chicago. The promontory on which it stands was named Grosse Point (Great Point) by early French fur traders in the seventeenth century.

Like these fur traders, early lake shipping followed the shoreline. Numerous ships were sunk off Grosse Point be-

Grosse Point Lighthouse.

cause of shallow water and turbulence created over shoals from high velocity winds. As a direct result, the Grosse Point Light Station was constructed. Still functioning, and licensed as a private aid to navigation by the U.S. Coast Guard, the site has played an important role in the maritime history of Chicago and northern Illinois. In recognition of this fact, the light station is listed in the National Register of Historic Places.

In addition to the 113-foot-tall light tower with adjoining passageway, the site comprises three buildings that are being adaptively reused to interpret the history of the light house and ecology of the area.

HAINES FARMHOUSE AND MUSEUM

1917 North Sheridan Road
Bowen Park
Waukegan, Illinois 60087
708/336-1859

Hours Wednesday–Friday, 10–2:30; Sunday, 1–3. Closed
Monday, Tuesday, and Saturday.
Admission Free.

The Haines Farmhouse and Museum, home of the
Waukegan Historical Society, features artifacts, photographs, and memorabilia pertinent to the Waukegan area.
The John Raymond Memorial Research Library contains a
variety of articles, books, photos, maps, and information
pertaining to Waukegan and Lake County.

HEDGES STATION

0N555 Winfield Road
Winfield, Illinois 60190
708/653-1489

Hours Vary.
Admission Free.

Hedges Station is the oldest remaining railroad depot in
Illinois. Built in 1849 to accommodate the Galena & Chicago
Union Railroad, the structure has served at various times as
a post office, general store, tavern, and residence. The building was moved from trackside to its present location by the

Winfield Historical Society, which is restoring it as a depot and general-store museum.

HIGHLAND PARK HISTORICAL SOCIETY

326 Central Avenue
Highland Park, Illinois 60035
708/432-7090

Hours Monday–Friday, 9–1 and afternoons by chance; Saturday, Sunday, and holidays, 2–4. Other times by appointment.
Admission Free.

The Highland Park Historical Society operates two museums and a bandstand. More than 6,000 items of local

Highland Park Historical Society Museum.

historical interest can be seen at the museums, including artifacts, clothing, antiques, furniture, photographs, glass slides, deeds, letters, plats, maps, newspapers, architectural drawings, and books.

The Jean Butz James Museum, at 326 Central Avenue, serves as headquarters for the society. The 10-room brick Victorian house, built in 1871, contains an 1880-period parlor, a library, a children's playroom with antique toys, and rooms depicting frontier life in the area, community history, and the history of Ravinia Park.

The Walt Durbahn Tool Museum is named after a longtime resident who gave his extensive collection of lumbering and carpentry tools to start the museum. It also contains tools from local trades and household items from the past.

The Francis Stupey Log Cabin is located in Laurel Park. Built in 1847, it is Highland Park's oldest structure. It has been restored and furnished in the period of 1850. The structure actually is a timber cabin made of hand-hewn squared timbers, dovetailed and notched at the joints, rather than round logs typical of a log cabin.

HISTORIC PULLMAN FOUNDATION

11111 South Forrestville Avenue
Chicago, Illinois 60628
312/785-8181

Hours Monday–Friday, 11–2; Saturday, 9–1; Sunday, 10–3.
Tours—May–October: the first Sunday of each month, 12:30 and 1:30, leaves from the Pullman Center. Special group tours available by appointment. Closed major holidays.
Guided Tours Adults, $3.50; senior citizens, $3; students, $2; children 12 and under, free.

A century ago, Pullman—the first planned industrial community built for workers—was considered to be "the world's most perfect town." Times have changed, but the 16-square block area on Chicago's Far South Side still is considered a historical and architectural national treasure.

Pullman was built in 1880–84 by George M. Pullman's Palace Car Company as a model industrial community. Believing that "man's productive powers and general usefulness to himself and society" could be improved by providing a desirable environment, Pullman decided to develop an eponymous town adjacent to his railroad–sleeping car works. The community was designed to sustain and uplift its residents with a school, parks, a church, markets, health services, a bank, recreational and cultural facilities, and housing for a broad socioeconomic range.

Under the supervision of architect Solon S. Beman and landscape architect Nathan F. Barrett, construction began in 1880 and the work progressed rapidly. The first six families moved into Pullman houses in January 1881, and the still-standing Hotel Florence—named for Pullman's daughter—welcomed its first guests in November of that year. By 1886, some 14,000 people lived in the town.

Prosperity and stability lasted until the depression of 1893–94 and the Pullman strike of 1894. Pullman reacted to unfavorable economic conditions by reducing wages without lowering rents in the company town. This helped to foster the notorious strike that led to the decline of the company and the community.

George Pullman died in 1897 and the following year the courts ordered the company to sell all its nonindustrial real estate. With the removal of company control, Pullman ceased to be a social experiment. In the years that followed, the community went through many changes. At times, Pullman's survival seemed doubtful. In 1960, the community was threatened with total destruction. But Pullman residents worked to defeat plans to turn the site into an industrial park. Efforts were intensified to restore the historic neighborhood, and Pullman was designated a city, state, and national historic landmark. The Historic Pullman Foundation was created in 1973 to carry on the preservation and rehabilitation of the area. Currently, the organization maintains the Historic Pullman Center and Market Hall and is in the process of bringing back the original elegance of the Hotel Florence.

Today, it is possible to visit the Hotel Florence and see Pullman's private suite and a number of other rooms at 11111 South Forrestville Avenue, where the Historic Pullman Foundation has its headquarters. Public tours begin at the Historic Pullman Center, 614 East 113th Street, with a multimedia presentation on the historic district. Originally a rooming house, the structure was taken over by the foundation. The tours also visit two major landmarks—the Hotel Florence and the historic Greenstone Church, the only church in Pullman.

Pullman has an annual house tour during the second weekend in October that includes visits to a sampling of the 600 buildings in the historic district. Each year the tour visits different houses, which are chosen to represent a cross-section of the original residential units and of the ways in which today's owners blend the past and present.

HISTORICAL SOCIETY OF OAK PARK AND RIVER FOREST

217 Home Avenue
Oak Park, Illinois 60302
708/848-6755

Hours Friday 10–2; Saturday–Sunday, 1–4. Closed
Monday–Thursday.
Admission Free.

Pleasant Home, formerly known as the Farson-Mills House,
is the site of this historical museum. The 1897 structure has
the style of Prairie School architecture, but was designed by
George W. Mather rather than Frank Lloyd Wright. Stained
glass windows, Victorian furniture, and glimpses of early
Oak Park/River Forest life, such as clothing, furnishings,
and toys, can be seen at the house.

ILLINOIS AND MICHIGAN CANAL MUSEUM

803 South State Street
Lockport, Illinois 60441
815/838-5080

Hours January–mid-December: daily,
1–4:30. Pioneer Settlement and Old Stone Annex Exhibits—April
16–October 1: daily, 1–4:30. Closed holidays and Thanksgiving
week.
Admission Free.

Parlor inside the Illinois and Michigan Canal Museum.

The Illinois and Michigan Canal opened in 1848 and operated until 1914. During its 66 years of operation, more than 10 million tons of commerce were carried on the 96-mile waterway that stretched from the south branch of the Chicago River to the Illinois River near LaSalle and Peru. The first of 15 locks was in Lockport, where the canal museum is located.

The Illinois and Michigan Canal Museum is housed in the canal's Office Building, built in 1837, which served as the office for the canal commissioners and the residence of the official in charge. In its earliest days, the canal office was considered second in importance to the capitol in Springfield as a state office.

Artifacts, documents, maps, and photographs relating to the history of the canal's construction and operation can be seen in the Canal Room. A kitchen, dining room, parlor, sewing room, and bedroom provide further insight into life during the canal period. Other highlights include the Commissioner's Office, a doctor's office, and the Will County History Room.

On the museum property operated by the Will County Historical Society, the Pioneer Settlement and the Old Stone

Annex Building also can be found. Among the 15 structures that are part of the complex are a one-room schoolhouse, blacksmith shop, log cabin, village jail, smoke house, tinsmith shop, settlement house, and railroad station.

JOLIET AREA HISTORICAL SOCIETY MUSEUM

17 E. Van Buren Street
Joliet, Illinois 60431
815/722-7003

Hours Tuesday–Friday, 12–3; Saturday, 10–2. Closed Sunday, Monday, New Year's Day, Fourth of July, Thanksgiving, day after Thanksgiving, and Christmas.
Admission Free.

The Joliet Area Historical Society Museum is a local history museum with exhibits that focus on Joliet-area industries, businesses, schools, people, and history. It also offers temporary exhibitions, lectures, and guided bike rides through historic areas.

KANKAKEE COUNTY HISTORICAL SOCIETY MUSEUM

Eighth Avenue and Water Street
Kankakee, Illinois 60901
815/932-5279

Hours Monday, Wednesday, Thursday, and Friday, 9–3; Saturday–Sunday, 1–4. Closed Tuesday.
Admission Free.

The Kankakee County Historical Society Museum occupies a three-building complex in Small Memorial Park in Kankakee. The facilities include the main Historical and Arts Building, the 1904 one-room Taylor School, and the restored 1800s home of Dr. A. L. Small, a pioneer physician in the area. The complex has six general exhibit areas—an Indian artifacts exhibit, a main gallery, a newspaper and print shop, the Centennial room, Taylor School, and Small home. A 7,500-square-foot addition, which has just been completed, will double the museum's space and offerings.

The museum's collections include housewares, period costumes, early firearms, period furniture, and historical records, books, photographs, letters, and manuscripts. The museum's historical library has a complete collection of local newspapers from 1867, thousands of photographs, and a valued collection of federally published Civil War documents.

KLINE CREEK FARM

1 N 600 County Farm Road
West Chicago, Illinois
708/970-4900, Ext. 304

Hours Thursday–Monday, 9–5. Closed Tuesday and Wednesday.
Admission Free.

The Kline Creek Farm, operated by the Forest Preserve District of DuPage County, shows farm life at the turn of the century. It is located on 1,000 acres in the Timber Ridge Forest Preserve near West Chicago. Interpreters in authentic costumes demonstrate daily chores.

The farm contains a number of buildings, such as the farmhouse, summer kitchen, barn, milk house, chicken coop, pump house, wagon shed, ice house, smokehouse, and sawdust bin. The farm is still growing and developing, with more farm buildings being planned and activities expanded.

KRUSE HOUSE MUSEUM

527 Main Street
West Chicago, Illinois 60185
708/231-0564/3376

Hours May–September: Saturday, 11–3. Group tours by appointment.
Admission Free.

This museum, operated by the West Chicago Historical Society, is located in the 1917 Kruse House and features the furnishings, household items, and collection of the Kruse family.

LAKE COUNTY MUSEUM

Route 176
Wanconda, Illinois 60084
708/526-7878

Hours Daily, 1–4:30. Closed New Year's Day, Thanksgiving, and Christmas.
Admission Adults, $1; students and senior citizens, 50¢; tours, in-county, 25¢; out-of-county, 40¢; children, free.

Materials related to Lake County's history can be seen at this museum. They include artifacts and exhibits from prehistoric to modern times, covering fields such as natural history, firearms, clothing, decorative arts, furniture, vehicles, paintings, and graphics. The museum also has the Curt Teich postcard collection available for research use, and an extensive library and archives pertaining to the area. It offers a variety of lecture, film, education, and hobby programming.

LANSING HISTORICAL SOCIETY AND MUSEUM

2750 Indiana Avenue
Lansing, Illinois 60438
708/474-6160

Hours Monday, 6 P.M.–8 P.M.; Wednesday, 10–12; Saturday, 2.
Admission Free.

This museum dealing with local history is located downstairs in the Lansing Public Library. It contains photographs, documents, and memorabilia from the area, and has a collection of First Lady dolls in inaugural gowns from Martha Washington to Nancy Reagan. In addition, the museum offers a display of Christmas trees from many lands and other holiday activities from November 19 through January 5 each year.

LIBERTYVILLE-MUNDELEIN HISTORICAL SOCIETY

413 North Milwaukee Avenue
Libertyville, Illinois 60048
708/362-2330

Hours Summer: Sunday, 2–4. Winter: by appointment.
Admission Free.

Housed in the 1876 Victorian residence of Ansel B. Cook, the museum contains artifacts, Civil War items, and historical books, photographs, maps, and papers from pioneer families of the area. Guided tours are available by contacting the society.

LOMBARD HISTORICAL SOCIETY

23 W. Maple
Lombard, Illinois 60148
708/629-1885

Hours Wednesday and Sunday, 1–4. Closed last two weeks in December.
Admission Adults, $1; senior citizens, 75¢; children 6–17, 50¢; children under 6, free.

Founded in 1970, the Lombard Historical Society is housed in an 1870s Victorian structure in Lombard that displays the life-style of a middle class family of that era. The society has collections of pre-1880 artifacts. It also sponsors an annual country fair, Christmas kaleidoscope, and ice-cream social.

Front Parlor, Lombard Historical Society.

McHENRY COUNTY HISTORICAL SOCIETY MUSEUM

6422 Main Street
Union, Illinois 60180
815/923-2267

Hours May–October: Wednesday, 1:30–4:30; June–August:
Wednesday, Saturday, and Sunday, 1:30–4:30.
Admission Adults, $3; children and senior citizens, $2.

A collection of artifacts that detail the history and growth of McHenry County can be seen at the museum, located in the 1870 Union School building. Among the objects on display are nineteenth-century musical instruments, clothing, handiwork, farm equipment, store furnishings, early products manufactured locally, and military memorabilia dating from the Civil War. An 1847 log cabin and an 1895 one-room schoolhouse also are part of the museum's offerings. The museum also has a local history research library, which is open year-round by appointment.

MORTON GROVE HISTORICAL MUSEUM

6240 Dempster Street
Morton Grove, Illinois 60053
708/965-0203

Hours Sunday, 2–4; special tours by arrangement.
Admission Free.

Haupt-Yehl House, Morton Grove Historical Museum.

The Morton Grove Historical Museum is located in the Haupt-Yehl House—a Victorian-style home built in 1888 that is typical of its times—in Harrer Park in Morton Grove. The museum has eight rooms, all furnished with authentic pieces of furniture of the period. Display cabinets are located in the basement area.

The museum is a cooperative effort of the Morton Grove Historical Society and the Morton Grove Park District.

NAPER SETTLEMENT MUSEUM VILLAGE

201 West Porter Avenue
Naperville, Illinois 60540
708/420-6010

Hours May–October: Wednesday, Saturday, and Sunday, 1:30–4:30.
Admission Adults, $4; children 6–17 and seniors, $2; children 5 and under, free.

Naper Settlement is a 12-acre nineteenth-century museum village located near downtown Naperville. It depicts an authentic northern Illinois town from the 1830s to the 1900s. Most of the 25 historical buildings are structures moved from other locations in the community.

The Century Memorial Chapel, constructed in 1864, was the first building moved to the village. Other structures include a 12-room Victorian mansion, print shop, blacksmith shop, and log house. Costumed guides lead tours and demonstrations in the various buildings.

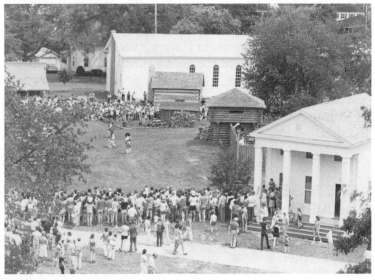

Naper Settlement.

ST. CHARLES HISTORICAL MUSEUM

2 East Main Street
St. Charles, Illinois 60174
708/584-6967

Hours Mid-February–December 23: Tuesday–Saturday, 12–4.
Closed Monday and other weeks of the year.
Admission Donation.

Operated by the St. Charles Historical Society, this local history museum has permanent and rotating exhibits on local and regional business, architecture, and community life-styles from 1834 to the present.

SEVEN ACRES ANTIQUE VILLAGE AND MUSEUM

8512 South Union Road
Union, Illinois 60180
815/923-2214

Hours May–September: daily, 9–6 (also open evenings
Friday–Saturday between Memorial Day and Labor Day); April
and October: weekends, 10–5. Closed November–March.
Admission Weekdays: adults, $4.50; senior citizens, $3.50;
children 5–12, $2.50; children under 5, free. Weekends: adults,
$5.50; senior citizens, $4.50; children 5–12, $3; children under 5,
free. Special group rates.

*Gunfights are staged daily on the western streets of Seven Acres Antique
Village.*

This unusual historical complex combines museum collections with a western village featuring live entertainment and operating stores. It was founded in 1974 by Larry Donley as a result of his great interest in antiques. His family still owns and operates the place. The museum has one of the nation's largest collections of Thomas Edison phonographs, as well as working-condition cylinder and disc music machines. Many military relics from World Wars I and II also can be seen. They include uniforms, medals, weapons, posters, flags, newspapers, and other such items. An old-time street offers an antique toy shop, clothing store, pawn shop, telegraph office, barber shop, doctor's office, and movie theater.

The village portion contains a general store, blacksmith shop, jail, saloon, pioneer cabin, garage, and gallows. Visitors can have their pictures taken in period clothes in the photography studio, get something to eat and drink at the ice-cream parlor and candy shop, see a resident craftsman restore old music machines in the phonograph repair shop, obtain a personalized "wanted" poster or gag newspaper at the print shop, play games in the antique arcade, and see live Wild West cowboy gunfight shows.

SOUTH HOLLAND HISTORICAL SOCIETY

6250 Wausau Avenue
South Holland, Illinois 60473
708/596-2722

Hours Saturday, 1–4. Closed rest of the week.
Admission Adults, $1; children, 50¢.

The South Holland Historical Society operates three sites: the Museum in the lower level of the Public Library; the

Barn on the Historical Paarlberg Farm, South Holland Historical Society.

Paarlberg Farm Homestead, built in 1870; and the Van Oostenbrugge Centennial Home, dating to 1858. The highlight of the museum is a diorama that depicts the area's business community in the late 1920s. It has more than 60 buildings.

STACY'S TAVERN

Main Street and Geneva Road
Glen Ellyn, Illinois 60137
708/858-8696

Hours Wednesday–Sunday, 1:30–4:30. Special tours by appointment. Closed mid-December–March 1.
Admission Adults, $1; students and children, 50¢.

In 1846 Moses Stacy built a new home for his family and an inn for travelers going to and from Chicago. The site became

Stacy's Tavern.

the birthplace of Glen Ellyn. The inn operated until 1892, when surviving son Philo Warren Stacy built a Victorian mansion at the site of his father's first log cabin. The village purchased Stacy's Tavern in 1968 and restored it with the help of the Glen Ellyn Historical Society and others. It was reopened as a museum in 1976 as part of the nation's bicentennial celebration. During the Christmas season, the tavern is decorated, entertainment is provided, and candlelight dinners are served by costumed volunteers.

WARRENVILLE HISTORICAL SOCIETY

3S 530 Second Street
Warrenville, Illinois 60555
708/393-4215

Hours March–December: Wednesday and Sunday, 1–4.
Closed January and February.
Admission Free.

The Albright Studio building, which dates back to 1858, serves as the home for the local history museum operated by the Warrenville Historical Society. Originally a church and school, the structure was used for a variety of purposes before becoming the Albright Gallery of Painting and Sculpture in 1924. After Adam Emory Albright's death in 1957, the building served as a studio, exhibition hall, theater, and office before being converted to a museum in 1984.

WAUKEGAN HISTORICAL SOCIETY

Bowen Park Haines Farmhouse
1917 North Sheridan Road
Waukegan, Illinois 60087
708/336-1859

Hours Wednesday–Friday, 10–2:30; Sunday, 1–3; and by special request. Seasonal open house programs in March, July, October, and December.
Admission Free.

A "farmhouse" once owned by two mayors that also was a country retreat for underprivileged city children is the home of the Waukegan Historical Society. Actually, the Bowen Park Haines Farmhouse never was primitive or rustic. It has a gracious interior that contains marble coal-burning fireplaces, doors with cut-glass scrollwork, and a built-in wardrobe that has been converted into a Lincoln Room.

Chicago Mayor John C. Haines retired to his Waukegan country house and died there in 1896. Waukegan Mayor Fred Buck purchased the property for a park in 1909, but never could gain enough support for the idea. In 1911, Mrs. Joseph T. Bowen, president and treasurer of the Hull-House settlement founded by Jane Addams, bought the property and converted it into a country retreat for underprivileged children. It was used for this purpose until acquired by the Waukegan Park District in 1973 and then leased to the historical society.

The Bowen Park Haines Farmhouse contains artifacts and memorabilia of Waukegan pioneers and descendants, a research and reference library, and the historical society's offices.

The society also operates a speakers' bureau and sponsors an annual "House Walk" on the third Sunday in May.

WEST CHICAGO HISTORICAL MUSEUM

132 Main Street
West Chicago, IL 60185
708/231-3376

Hours Wednesday–Friday, 1–4; Saturday, 11–3; or by appointment.
Admission Free.

The West Chicago Historical Museum is housed in two buildings: the 1884 former Town Hall and Fire Station and the 1890 Chicago, Burlington & Quincy Station. The railroad station and a caboose are part of "Heritage Commons," a small railroad park. The museum's collections include railroad memorabilia and equipment, woodworking tools and farm implements, and documents and photographs pertaining to local history.

Western Springs Historical Society.

WESTERN SPRINGS HISTORICAL SOCIETY

Tower Green
PO Box 139
Western Springs, Illinois 60558
708/246-9230

Hours Saturday, 10–2; Thursday in summer, 7 P.M.–9 P.M.
Admission Free.

The Western Springs Historical Society operates a museum in the 112-foot-high stone Water Tower, built in 1892 on the village green. Among the permanent exhibits are objects and photographs from the community's first homes, families, and celebrations; furniture, pictures, and documents that record the Chicago, Burlington & Quincy Railroad's role in the development of Western Springs; and a partial reproduction of Henrikson's general store. In addition, the museum has scheduled temporary exhibitions on such topics as Indian life in the area, Victorian styles, and toys and dolls at Christmas time.

WILMETTE HISTORICAL MUSEUM

565 Hunter Road
Wilmette, Illinois 60091
708/256-5838

Hours Tuesday, Wednesday, and Thursday, 9:30–12 and 1:30–4; Saturday–Sunday, 2–5; first Monday of month, 7:30 P.M.–9 P.M.; other hours by appointment. Closed July and August.
Admission Free.

A Brownie troop visits the Wilmette Historical Museum.

Wilmette history from pre-Columbian Indians through the village centennial is displayed at this museum, located in a wing of a former school and operated by the Village of Wilmette with support from the Wilmette Historical Society and other sources. Changing exhibits can be seen in the Costume Room. Temporary exhibitions on topics of local and/or current interest also are presented from time to time.

WINNETKA HISTORICAL MUSEUM

1140 Elm Street
Winnetka, Illinois 60093
708/501-6025

Hours Tuesday, Thursday, and Saturday, 1–4.
Admission Free.

In 1986 the Village of Winnetka and the Winnetka Historical Society founded the Winnetka Historical Museum, located in a landmark school building. It contains historical information, memorabilia, and artifacts relating to the village.

Among the 8,000 items in the collections are photographs, paintings, books, clothing, models of old Winnetka buildings, recorded oral histories, films, and various other materials. Especially noteworthy is the Carleton Washburne Memorial Library, a leading educator's collection on loan from the school district.

Among the special exhibitions presented at the museum have been "Winnetka's First Fifty Years," "Marshall Fields of 1885," "Winnetka Architecture: Where Past Is Present," and most recently, an exhibition on Winnetka schools.

ZION HISTORICAL SOCIETY

1300 Shiloh Boulevard
Zion, Illinois 60099
708/746-2427

Hours June–August: Saturday–Sunday, 2–5; other times by appointment.
Admission Adults, $1; children, 50¢.

The Zion Historical Society is located in the 1902 Shiloh House, residence of the founder of the City of Zion. It contains some original furnishings, antiques, religious artifacts, and various manuscripts.

MEDICAL AND HEALTH MUSEUMS

Medical and health museums are concerned with medical history or health education. The International Museum of Surgical Science and Wood Library Museum of Anesthesiology fall in the historical category, while the Robert Crown Center for Health Education is an exponent of the latter.

Exhibits dealing with medicine and health also can be found at the Museum of Science and Industry, which devotes much of its balcony level to participatory displays explaining human development; health awareness; and the nature, prevention, and treatment of various health problems.

Also see:

Museum of Science and Industry (The Big Three)

ROBERT CROWN CENTER FOR HEALTH EDUCATION

21 Salt Creek Lane
Hinsdale, Illinois 60521
708/325-1000

Hours Mid-September–mid-June: Monday–Friday, 9:45–2:30
(for school groups only); others, 2:30–4. Closed major holidays.
Admission Kindergarten–grade 2, $1.75; grade 3 and up, $2;
individuals and other groups, $1.25 to $2 after hours.

This health education center, once known as the Hinsdale
Health Museum, seeks to further healthful behavior
primarily through organized instructional programs for
schools, youth organizations, and adult groups.

Its medical and health exhibits and special classrooms are
used as teaching tools in scheduled classes dealing with
general health, birth, family living, the environment, human
ecology, drug abuse, nutrition, and professional health
education.

Twenty-seven programs are related to school curricula.
They are designed to augment regular classroom instruction
for kindergarten to fifth grade, middle/junior high school,
and senior high-school students enrolled in biology, general
science, geography, health, home economics, and sociology
courses.

The Crown Center also has an after-hours program for
individuals, family groups, and nonschool groups. Presentations begin between 2:30 and 4 P.M., depending on the program, and last from a half hour to one and a half hours.
Reservations are required.

INTERNATIONAL MUSEUM OF SURGICAL SCIENCE

International College of Surgeons
1524 North Lake Shore Drive
Chicago, Illinois 60610
708/642-3555

Hours Tuesday–Saturday, 10–4; Sunday, 11–5. Closed Monday.
Admission Free.

The story of healing from medicine man to modern surgeon can be seen at this unique historical museum operated by the International College of Surgeons, whose members represent virtually every country in the world.

Founded in 1956 by Dr. Max Thorek, the museum has 32 exhibit halls showing the development of many surgical specialties, such as obstetrics and gynecology, orthopedics, urology, and radiology, and rooms pertaining to surgical history, instruments, and accomplishments in various countries, including Austria, Brazil, China, France, Greece, Israel, Italy, Japan, and Spain.

Among the artifacts on display are trephining tools used by the Mayans, Incas, and Aztecs; a thirteenth-century anatomical chart showing a human with two hearts; a model of a 1594 anatomical theater; one of Florence Nightingale's nurse caps of white lace; the original apparatus used in the Carrel-Lindbergh heart experimentation; the first stethoscope; a 1920s iron lung; and Napoleon's death mask.

The museum also offers an early American apothecary shop; oil paintings depicting surgical procedures, anesthesia, and anatomy; a memorial room dedicated to Dr. Thorek; and the Hall of Immortals with its 12 eight-foot-high stone-cast sculptures of such early exponents of surgical

International College of Surgeons.

science as Hippocrates, Louis Pasteur, William Harvey, Marie Curie, and Wilhelm Roentgen.

WOOD LIBRARY—MUSEUM OF ANESTHESIOLOGY

515 Busse Highway
Park Ridge, Illinois 60068
708/825-5586

Hours Monday–Friday, 9–4:30. Closed weekends and holidays.
Admission Free.

The medical history of anesthesiology is featured in this facility located in the executive office of the American Society of Anesthesiologists. The collections include anesthesia equipment and manuscripts. An 8,000-volume library on anesthesiology also is available.

MILITARY MUSEUMS

Military history is the focus of two museums in the Chicago area—the Fort Sheridan Museum and the Grand Army of the Republic Memorial and Veteran's Military Museum. Historical documents, photographs, and objects relating to the Fifth Army, the Civil War, and the two World Wars can be seen at these museums.

Three museums described in other sections also have exhibits related to the military services. The First Division Museum is part of Cantigny. The Museum of Science and Industry has exhibits dealing with the Air Force, Navy, and Army Corps of Engineers. It also is possible to see historic aircraft and to tour the U-505, a German submarine captured during World War II, at the science museum.

Also see:

Cantigny (Major Museums and Similar Institutions)
Museum of Science and Industry (The Big Three)

FORT SHERIDAN MUSEUM

Building 33
Fort Sheridan, Illinois 60037
708/926-2173

Hours Daily, 10–4. Closed holidays.
Admission Free.

This military museum is located in a one-story building originally designed as a post stockade by William Holabird. It is one structure in a 94-building national historic landmark district. It traces Army and Fort Sheridan history through collections of firearms, uniforms, soldier gear and supplies, maps, photographs, and objects relating to life at the post.

GRAND ARMY OF THE REPUBLIC MEMORIAL AND VETERAN'S MILITARY MUSEUM

23 East Downer Place
Aurora, Illinois 60505
708/897-7221

Hours Monday, Wednesday, and Friday, 12–4. Closed Tuesday, Thursday, and weekends.
Admission Free.

Military collections from the Civil, Spanish-American, Korean, Vietnam, and two World Wars are displayed in an 1877 octagon-shaped sandstone building that was the post home of the Grand Army of the Republic for 65 years. A library of war history consists mostly of Civil War books.

NATURAL HISTORY MUSEUMS, CONSERVATORIES, AND NATURE CENTERS

The Chicago area has a broad range of institutions concerned with natural history, the environment, and the animal world. Many of these organizations, such as the Field Museum of Natural History, Chicago Botanic Garden, Garfield and Lincoln Park conservatories, Morton Arboretum, and Brookfield and Lincoln Park zoos, are covered in other sections.

This section is concerned largely with an array of nature centers, mostly small and local in scope, which number 14. In general, they are operated by suburban park districts, county forest preserves, and environmental groups. In some instances, they include historic houses and involve historical societies.

Also see:

Brookfield Zoo (Major Museums and Similar Institutions)
Chicago Academy of Sciences (Major Museums and Similar Institutions)
Chicago Botanic Garden (Major Museums and Similar Institutions)
Field Museum of Natural History (The Big Three)
Garfield Park Conservatory (Major Museums and Similar Institutions)
Lincoln Park Conservatory (Major Museums and Similar Institutions)

Lincoln Park Zoological Gardens (Major Museums and Similar Institutions)
Morton Arboretum (Major Museums and Similar Institutions)
John G. Shedd Aquarium (Major Museums and Similar Institutions)

Crabtree Nature Center.

CRABTREE NATURE CENTER

Palatine Road
Barrington, Illinois 60010
708/381-6592

Hours Summer: Monday–Thursday, 9–4:30; Saturday, Sunday, and holidays, 9–5; winter: daily, 9–4. Closed Friday, New Year's Day, Thanksgiving, and Christmas.
Admission Free.

This facility is one of five nature centers operated as part of the Cook County Forest Preserve District. The nature center, which covers over a thousand acres, has an exhibit building and several miles of self-guiding trails.

ELGIN PUBLIC MUSEUM

225 Grand Boulevard
Elgin, Illinois 60120
708/741-6655

Hours Memorial Day–Labor Day: Tuesday–Sunday, 12–4; September–late November and mid-January–Memorial Day: Saturday–Sunday, 12–4.
Admission Adults, $1; senior citizens and children, 25¢; children under 3, free.

The Elgin Public Museum, located in a 1907 neoclassical building in a 120-acre municipal park, is a natural history museum. It contains a variety of specimens in the fields of anthropology, botany, zoology, ornithology, geology, and paleontology, including endangered and extinct species.

The museum also has Native American objects, Illinois wildlife specimens, experimental teaching materials, and a 500-volume natural history research library.

FABYAN MUSEUM

1511 South Batavia Avenue
Geneva, Illinois 60134
708/232-4811

Hours May–mid-October: Saturday, Sunday, and holidays, 1–5; other times by appointment.
Admission Free.

The Fabyan Museum is located in the 235-acre Fabyan Forest Preserve operated by Kane County along the Fox River in Geneva. The museum, housed in the 1907 "Riverbank" villa of the late Col. George Fabyan that was designed by Frank Lloyd Wright, contains mounted animals, Oriental artifacts, and a collection of historic photographs. The former Fabyan estate also has a Dutch windmill, a Japanese tea garden, and a lighthouse.

Fabyan, who became wealthy in the cotton textile business, conducted pioneering research in acoustics, cryptology, physical fitness, livestock breeding, and plant genetics in his laboratories. The Riverbank Laboratories, located on the west side of Route 31, now are used for acoustic research and development by the Illinois Institute of Technology and its affiliate, IIT Research Institute, under a Fabyan trust.

FULLERSBURG WOODS NATURE CENTER

3609 Spring Road
Oak Brook, Illinois 60521
708/790-4900, weekdays; 790-4912, weekends.

Hours Environmental Center—daily, 9–5. Closed winter weekends and holidays. Nature Preserve—daily, one hour after sunrise to one hour after sunset.
Admission Free.

The Fullersburg Woods Nature Center is part of the 206-acre Fullersburg Woods Forest Preserve operated by DuPage County. In 1973 the badly degraded and overused forest preserve was chosen to demonstrate what special management can do to help an area return to a more natural state. The interpretation center is the focal point of this opportunity to view wildlife in a natural setting and learn about environmental relationships in the rapidly urbanizing county.

The nature center features a 20-minute sound and slide show in the Environmental Theater, lifelike displays and colorful dioramas in the Environmental Gallery, a wetland ecosystem with sights and sounds in the Samuel Dean Memorial Marsh, and a two-kilometer sound-interpreted hiking trail that winds through the preserve.

THE GROVE

1421 Milwaukee Avenue
Glenview, Illinois 60025
708/299-6096

Hours Monday–Friday, 8–4:30; Kennicott House—Sunday, 1–4.
Admission Free. Kennicott House—person, $1.50; family, $3.

A national historic landmark, The Grove is a museum and a nature preserve operated by the Glenview Park District. Three historic houses—the Kennicott House, the Redfield Center, and the Interpretive Center—can be seen at the 82-acre park that has miles of beautiful hiking trails.

Kennicott House at The Grove.

The Grove was settled by the pioneering Kennicott family in 1836. The Kennicott House, built in 1856, recently was restored to its original condition. Dr. John Kennicott and his family were active in a number of activities of historical significance, including popularizing interest in nature, developing horticulture in Illinois, founding the Chicago Academy of Sciences, establishing agricultural colleges through the land grant system, collecting samples for the Smithsonian Institution, and exploring Alaska and Central America.

The Redfield Center was the home of descendants of the Kennicott settlers. The house, constructed in 1929 to replace one that burned, was designed by George C. Elmslie, a follower of the Louis Sullivan School of Chicago Architecture. The Redfield Center and the Interpretive Center serve as the heart of a year-round historic, environmental, and cultural program.

WALTER E. HELLER NATURE PARK AND INTERPRETIVE CENTER

2821 Ridge Road
Highland Park, Illinois 60035
708/433-6901

Hours Monday–Friday, 8:30–5; Saturday–Sunday, 12–5. Closed holidays.
Admission Free.

This interpretive center operated by the Park District of Highland Park is located in the 97-acre Walter E. Heller Nature Park in the middle of Chicago's northern suburbs. It contains lobby displays, a discovery room with participatory exhibits, a reference library, and other facilities, and it offers a variety of environmental education programs.

Heller Nature Center.

The nature park has several natural communities, including hardwoods and pine forests, prairies, and a pond. In addition, three miles of marked trails, a log cabin, and a shaded picnic area with tables and fire grates can be found at the park.

JURICA NATURAL HISTORY MUSEUM

Illinois Benedictine College
5700 College Road
Lisle, Illinois 60532
708/960-1500

Hours Monday–Friday, Sunday, and holidays, 10–3; special tours by appointment.
Admission Free.

Jurica Natural History Museum. (photo by G. Czerak)

A mounted duck-billed platypus, a grizzly bear, an orangutan, two chimpanzees, an African buffalo, and an impressive collection of skeletons—dominated by a 38-foot Rorqual whale—are among the specimens that can be seen at the Jurica Natural History Museum at Illinois Benedictine College near Lisle.

The museum, named for the Reverend Hilary S. Jurica, O.S.B., founder and longtime biology professor at the college, occupies 3,800 square feet in the Dr. William Scholl Science Center. The Reverend Hilary S. Jurica and his brother, the Reverend Edmund Jurica, O.S.B., assembled the thousands of specimens on display in the museum that have been used as teaching tools in biology over the last half century.

LADD ARBORETUM AND ECOLOGY CENTER

Evanston Environmental Association
2024 McCormick Boulevard
Evanston, Illinois 60201
708/864-5181

Hours Ladd Arboretum—at all times. Ecology Center—Tuesday–Saturday, 9–4:30.
Admission Free.

The Ladd Arboretum and Ecology Center are operated by the Evanston Environmental Association, which also is responsible for the Grosse Point Lighthouse Park that includes the Grosse Point Light Station, Lighthouse Nature Center, Visitor/Maritime Center, and Margery Carlson Educational Greenhouse (see Historical Museums and Houses).

Named in memory of Edward Rixon Ladd, founder, publisher, and editor of the *Evanston Review*, the arboretum stretches along McCormick Boulevard on a narrow 23-acre strip of reclaimed land along the North Shore Channel. Among the highlights are the Rotary International Friendship Garden, Cherry Tree Walk, Women's Terrace, bird sanctuary, and prairie restoration area.

Environmental programs are presented at the Ecology Center, located at the Ladd Arboretum. It also is the site of workshops, classes, nature programs, and the Evanston Environmental Association offices.

LILACIA PARK

Lombard Park District
150 South Park
Lombard, Illinois 60148
708/627-1281

Hours Daily, 9–9.
Admission Adults, $1.50; senior citizens, $1; children, free.

The Lombard Park District operates this botanical garden with 8½ acres of lilac plantings and an 1888 coach house. It offers guided tours, lectures, and films.

Little Red Schoolhouse Nature Center.

LITTLE RED SCHOOLHOUSE NATURE CENTER

Willow Springs Road at 104th Avenue
Willow Springs, Illinois 60480
708/839-6897

Hours Summer: Monday–Thursday, 9–4:30; Saturday, Sunday, and holidays, 9–5. Winter (November–February): daily, 9–4. Closed Friday, New Year's Day, Thanksgiving, and Christmas.
Admission Free.

An 1886 schoolhouse serves as a nature center for the Cook County Forest Preserve District in the Palos Hills area. It contains exhibits on nature, history, and live native animals. A garden, waterfowl feeding area, wildflowers, prairie restoration, and an orchard can be found outside the building.

NORTHERN ILLINOIS UNIVERSITY ANTHROPOLOGY MUSEUM

Stevens Building
Northern Illinois University
DeKalb, Illinois 60115
815/753-0230

Hours Monday–Friday, 9–5. Closed weekends and university holidays.
Admission Free.

Founded in 1964, the Anthropology Museum at Northern Illinois University in DeKalb is a departmental museum with excellent collections of ethnographic, archaeological, and physical anthropological materials from Southeast Asia, New Guinea, the Plains Indians, and elsewhere.

Demonstration Garden, the North Park Village Nature Center.

NORTH PARK VILLAGE NATURE CENTER

5801 North Pulaski Road
Chicago, Illinois 60646
312/583-8970 and 583-3714

Hours Daily, 10–4. Closed holidays.
Admission Free.

This nature center is part of a larger North Park Village complex managed by Chicago's Department of Public Works that also includes a community health center, two elderly housing units, a park, and a learning center.

The site has had a long and colorful history. One of its first owners was Chief Sauganash, perhaps the best-known local Native American. The City of Chicago purchased the 154-acre tract in 1911 from Pehr Peterson, who operated a tree nursery and provided much of the original landscaping. For more than 60 years, the Metropolitan Tuberculosis Sanitarium was located there before being phased out in 1974. Commercial development of the property was opposed by local residents, who persuaded the city to adopt a plan that maintains the integrity of the site, recycles some of the sanitarium buildings, and preserves most of the natural areas.

The North Park Village Nature Center building was renovated in 1985 and today has a growing collection of natural history exhibits, a library, demonstration gardens, an apiary, and a variety of environmental education activities. Visitors also can use the trail system through a 46-acre preserve being restored to prairie and oak savanna and see a 15-acre nature study area.

OAK PARK CONSERVATORY

615 Garfield Street
Oak Park, Illinois 60304
708/386-4700

Hours Monday, 2–4; Tuesday–Sunday, 10–4.
Admission Free.

The Oak Park Conservatory, operated by the Oak Park Park District, has a cacti and succulent collection in the Desert

Room, exotic tropical plants in the Tropical Room, and subtropical plants and seasonal floral shows in the Fern Room. It has native prairie, herb, and gazebo gardens, as well as a library, classroom, guided tours, films, lectures, and organized education programs.

PREHISTORIC LIFE MUSEUM

704 Main Street
Evanston, Illinois 60202
708/866-7374

Hours Monday–Tuesday and Thursday–Friday, 10:30–5:40; Saturday, 10–5. Closed Wednesday and Sunday.
Admission Free.

Fossils from every geologic time period, including an extensive display of fossils from Illinois, can be seen at the Prehistoric Life Museum, a privately owned facility in Evanston.

RIVER TRAIL NATURE CENTER

3120 West Milwaukee Avenue
Northbrook, Illinois 60062
708/824-8360

Hours Summer: Monday–Thursday, 9–4:30; Saturday, Sunday, and holidays, 9–5. Winter: daily, 9–4. Closed Friday, New Year's Day, Thanksgiving, and Christmas.
Admission Free.

Native birds, mammals, fish, amphibians, and reptiles are exhibited at this nature center in the Des Plaines River Valley operated by the Cook County Forest Preserve District. The center also has an organic garden, an herb garden, a honeybee colony, an orchard, seasonal exhibits, three self-guiding nature trails, and children's and family programs throughout the year.

River Trail Nature Center.

Edward L. Ryerson Conservation Area.

EDWARD L. RYERSON CONSERVATION AREA

**21950 North Riverwoods Road
Deerfield, Illinois 60015
708/948-7750**

Hours Daily, 8:30–5.
Admission Free.

The Edward L. Ryerson Conservation Area is a 550-acre plant and wildlife sanctuary in Lake County, with 300 acres designated as the Illinois Nature Preserve. The natural beauty of the area has changed little since Potowatomi Chief

Mettawa helped the first European settler, Daniel Wright, build his cabin near the site in 1834.

In 1928, Edward and Nora Ryerson built a small log cabin along the Des Plaines River near a spot where two major Indian trails once crossed the river. In 1939, the Ryersons purchased the land north of their cabin and began developing their "Bushwood Farm." By 1942, they completed their Greek revival-style house, which now serves as the Ryerson Woods Visitors Center.

Edward Ryerson was involved in the formation of the Lake County Forest Preserve District in 1958, and in 1966 his family began donating the deciduous bottomland forest to the district. In 1972, the Forest Preserve District became owner of the property, which serves as the education center for the county's forest preserves. In addition to the educational activities in the house and surrounding area, visitors can see natural history displays in the Exhibit Cabin, agricultural exhibits in the Farm Barns, and river exhibits in the Smith River Cabin, as well as the Ryerson Cabin and Dam. Self-guided trail tours are available. Reservations also can be made for guided nature walks and programs for children and adults.

SAND RIDGE NATURE CENTER

Paxton Avenue
South Holland, Illinois 60473
708/868-0606

Hours Summer: Monday–Thursday, 9–4:30; Saturday, Sunday, and holidays, 9–5. Winter: daily, 9–4. Closed Friday, New Year's Day, Thanksgiving, and Christmas.
Admission Free.

Sand Ridge Nature Center.

Sand Ridge Nature Center emphasizes the natural history of the Calumet region and its relation to the geological past. Exhibits, three nature trails, and a garden are part of this facility operated by the Forest Preserve District of Cook County.

SPRING VALLEY NATURE SANCTUARY

1111 East Schaumburg Road
Schaumburg, Illinois 60194
708/980-2100

Hours Grounds and trails—8–sunset. Visitor Center—9–5.
Closed New Year's Day and Christmas.
Admission Free.

Spring Valley Nature Sanctuary.

Spring Valley Nature Sanctuary is a 135-acre "living museum" operated by the Schaumburg Park District. Its woodlands, marshes, streams, and restored prairies are being preserved for wildlife conservation and environmental education. In addition to 3½ miles of hiking trails, the site contains an earth-sheltered visitor center. Among the attractions here are natural history displays, a library, greenhouses, classroom areas, and an observation tower. A log cabin on the site is open on weekends for food preparation demonstrations of the period. Historic interpretation also is conducted at an 1880s living history farm.

TRAILSIDE MUSEUM OF NATURAL HISTORY

738 Thatcher Avenue
River Forest, Illinois 60305
708/366-6530

Hours Daily, 10–12 and 1–4. Closed Thursday, New Year's Day, Thanksgiving, and Christmas.
Admission Free.

This Cook County Forest Preserve District nature center occupies an 1870s-vintage house along the banks of the Des Plaines River. It contains displays and animals, but does not have any nature trails.

WILLOWBROOK WILDLIFE HAVEN

Willowbrook Forest Preserve
Park Boulevard between Roosevelt and Butterfield Roads
Glen Ellyn, Illinois 60137
708/790-4913

Hours Daily, 9–5. Closed New Year's Day, Thanksgiving, and Christmas.
Admission Free.

The DuPage County Forest Preserve District operates this wildlife park on 43 acres of gently rolling land in the heart of the suburban county. The property was donated to the district in 1956 by Mrs. Audie Chase, who wished that the area be maintained as a wildlife sanctuary. Two years later, the

Willowbrook Wildlife Haven.

district permitted Richard and Dorothy Hoger to establish a basic facility to treat injured and helpless animals.

Over the years Willowbrook has grown, and now more than 4,000 animals are treated and approximately 50,000 people visit the wildlife preserve each year. The nature center serves as a learning resource and local authority on native animals, a hospital and rehabilitation center for injured and immature wildlife, and a facility for public enjoyment through films, lectures, demonstrations, and guided tours.

Of specific interest is Willowbrook's collection of more than 100 permanently disabled birds and mammals in indoor and outdoor exhibit areas. Visitors can enjoy "Opossum Hollow," a museum discovery room with hands-on natural history specimens. Exhibits also include an interpretive nature trail and a model backyard, landscaped with the needs of wildlife in mind.

In the spring and summer, visitors can view orphaned animals through a special window at the center's nursery. Informational brochures also are available at the center.

RELIGIOUS MUSEUMS

Museums concerned with religious history, beliefs, and activities are becoming more common. Three such institutions can be found in the Chicago area—Bahá'í House of Worship, Billy Graham Center Museum, and Morton B. Weiss Museum of Judaica.

These facilities are primarily information centers for various denominations, tracing their development, containing religious artifacts, and serving as places of worship. They usually are part of a larger religious complex.

Also see:

Spertus Museum of Judaica (Ethnic Museums)

BAHÁ'Í HOUSE OF WORSHIP

Linden Avenue
Wilmette, Illinois 60091
708/256-4400

Hours May–September: daily, 10–10. October–April: daily, 10–5.
Admission Free.

The Bahá'í Temple is more than a house of worship, it's an architectural marvel. It took more than 50 years to complete the unusual structure adorned with hundreds of intricate cast concrete panels.

Bahá'í House of Worship. (photo by Fred G. Korth)

The auditorium, with its walls of lace-like ornamentation, has a dome that rises 138 feet above the main floor. It is one of the tallest unobstructed interiors of any building.

A visitor's center on the lower level offers several slide presentations and informational displays on the Bahá'í Faith. The gardens also are open to the public.

BILLY GRAHAM CENTER MUSEUM

Wheaton College
500 East Seminary Avenue
Wheaton, Illinois 60187
708/260-5909

Hours Monday–Saturday, 9:30–5:30; Sunday, 1–5. Closed holidays.
Admission Adults, $2; children, 50¢.

Part of the Billy Graham Center at Wheaton College, this museum presents a visual history of the growth of evangelism in the United States. The exhibits trace evangelism from colonial church leaders through the ministry of recent American evangelists, including the Reverend Billy Graham, and climax with a presentation of the gospel.

The museum tour begins in the "Rotunda of Witnesses," where large wall hangings depict great religious leaders from the past and the present. In the "Evangelism in America" hall, the development of evangelism in America is shown through artifacts, dioramas, and exhibits. The next section deals with the growth and role of the Billy Graham Evangelistic Association. The concluding "Walk Through the Gospel" exhibit, which uses sights and sounds to communicate the story of the gospel, is followed by a visit to the chapel.

MORTON B. WEISS MUSEUM OF JUDAICA

K.A.M. Isaiah Israel Congregation
1100 Hyde Park Boulevard
Chicago, Illinois 60615
312/924-1234

Hours Monday–Friday, 10–4; Sunday, 10–12 during school year. Closed Saturday.
Admission Free.

A collection of religious and cultural artifacts can be seen at K.A.M. Isaiah Israel, the oldest Jewish congregation in the

Morton B. Weiss Museum of Judaica. (photo by Steve Grubman)

Midwest. The congregation, which dates back to 1847, is located in a landmark Byzantine-style sanctuary designed by architect Alfred S. Alschuler in 1924.

Among the objects on display at the museum are a 300-year-old white-jade Chinese mezzuzah, a tenth-century silver Spanish Purim megillah, an eighteenth-century Oriental Torah and Torah case from an Egyptian synagogue, a Hebrew edition of the Bible printed in Antwerp in 1574, matrimonial contracts written on parchment, and silver, ivory, and wood spice boxes.

SCIENCE, TECHNOLOGY, AND INDUSTRIAL MUSEUMS

Museums in this category come in many varieties—scientific, technological, industrial, and various specialties. The largest of these institutions are the Museum of Science and Industry, Field Museum of Natural History, and Adler Planetarium, which are described in other sections. The facilities in this section are 12 specialized museums dealing essentially with a single field. They include such diverse places as the Cernan Earth and Space Center, Chicago Maritime Museum, Illinois Railway Museum, Museum of Broadcast Communications, Museum of Holography/Chicago, Volo Antique Auto Museum and Village, and the new Science and Technology Interactive Center.

Also see:

**Adler Planetarium (Major Museums and Similar
Institutions)**

**Chicago Academy of Sciences (Major Museums and
Similar Institutions)**

**Robert Crown Center for Health Education (Medical
and Health Museums)**

Field Museum of Natural History (The Big Three)

**Graue Mill and Museum (Historic Museums and
Houses)**

**Great Lakes Naval and Maritime Museum (Military
Museums)**

**Illinois and Michigan Canal Museum (Historic
Museums and Houses)**

International Museum of Surgical Science (Medical and Health Museums)
Museum of Science and Industry (The Big Three)
Seven Acres Antique Village and Museum (Historic Museums and Houses)
Wood Library—Museum of Anesthesiology (Medical and Health Museums)

CERNAN EARTH AND SPACE CENTER

2000 North Fifth Avenue
River Grove, Illinois 60171
708/456-5815

Hours Monday, 9–5; Tuesday–Thursday, 9–9; Friday 9–10; Saturday, 1–10; Sunday, 1–4. Closed New Year's Day, Easter, Thanksgiving, and Christmas.
Admission Adults, $4; children and senior citizens, $2. Laser show: adults, $5; children and senior citizens, $2.50.

Affiliated with Triton College, the Cernan Earth and Space Center is a planetarium with sky shows, Cinema-360 big-screen films, laser light shows, space exhibits, and educational programming that includes classes, lectures, teleconferences, and concerts. The collections include meteorites and space hardware of historical interest, while special exhibitions usually deal with astronomy and space exploration.

CHICAGO MARITIME MUSEUM

465 East Illinois Street
Chicago, Illinois 60611
312/943-9090

Hours Tuesday–Sunday, 12–5. Closed Monday.
Admission Adults, $1.

Founded in 1982, the Chicago Maritime Museum is operated
by the Chicago Maritime Society and is housed in the 1905
North Pier Terminal. The emphasis is on Great Lakes and
inland waterways maritime history.

The museum's collections include canoes, small
watercraft, paintings, photographs, manuscripts, and other
materials. It also has a 7-foot scale replica of *Ra II*, a 1940s Old
Town sailing dinghy, and a 1939, 26-foot Coast Guard rescue
surf boat.

Activities include guided tours, lectures, films, concerts,
arts festivals, education programs, and the annual Maritime
Folk Festival.

FOX RIVER TROLLEY MUSEUM

Illinois Route 31
South Elgin, Illinois 60177
708/697-4676

Hours Second Sunday of May–first Sunday in November:
Sunday, 11–6. July–August: also Saturday, 12–5.
Admission Free. Trolley rides—adults, $2; senior citizens, $1.50;
children, $1.

Chicago Aurora & Elgin car #20, built in 1902 to run on the Aurora Elgin & Fox River interurban line south of South Elgin, Illinois. (photo by J. R. Hazinski)

A three-mile ride on an authentic 1896 electric railway is part of the experience at this trolley museum. An assortment of electric railway vehicles from an 1895 street-railway post-office car to a 1947 articulated rapid transit train round out the 19-unit collection.

HAEGER MUSEUM

7 Maiden Lane
Dundee, Illinois 60118
708/426-3441

Hours Monday–Friday, 8:30–5; Saturday, Sunday, and holidays, 10–5. Closed New Year's Day, Easter, Thanksgiving, and Christmas.
Admission Free.

This corporate museum is part of the outlet store at Haeger Potteries. Its exhibits show the evolution of the company from its inception as a brick and tile manufacturer in 1871 to its present position as a leading manufacturer of decorative accessories and lamps.

Haeger, which operated a working factory at the 1933–34 Century of Progress Exposition in Chicago, still offers a free plant tour. The world's largest art pottery vase, produced by Haeger, is on display in the museum.

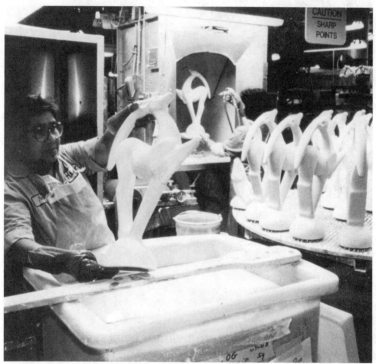

The Haeger Potteries Production Area, as viewed from the Haeger Museum.

Inside Hartung's Automotive Museum.

HARTUNG'S AUTOMOTIVE MUSEUM

3623 West Lake Street
Glenview, Illinois 60025
708/724-4354

Hours Daily, but vary.
Admission Donation.

More than 100 antique automobiles, trucks, tractors, and motorcycles are displayed at Hartung's Automotive Museum. They include such early car models as the 1922 Studebaker, 1926 Hertz Touring, and 1927 Henney Limousine; trucks like the 1914 Ford stake truck and 1929 Ford one-ton truck; and vintage motorcycles such as the 1901

Wagner, 1905 Fabrique-Nationale, and 1908 Thor and Excelsior.

The museum also has 75 antique bicycles and one of the finest license plate collections anywhere. Other collections on exhibit deal with promotional model cars, antique hub caps, radiator emblems, auto mascots, spark plugs, tools, gas engines, and farm machinery.

ILLINOIS RAILWAY MUSEUM

Olson Road
Union, Illinois 60180
815/923-4000

Hours Memorial Day–Labor Day: daily, 10–5. May, September, and October: weekends, 10–5. Closed November–April.
Admission Adults, $5.50; children, $2.75, when steam trains operate; adults, $4.50, children, $2.25, all other times.

Some 225 pieces of equipment, including steam and diesel locomotives, trolleys, streetcars, interurban cars, rapid transit cars, railroad passenger coaches, and other rolling stock, can be seen at the Illinois Railway Museum, which also offers rides on its demonstration railroad.

An 1851 rail depot (from Marengo, Illinois) is the focal point of this railway museum that occupies 56 acres. It is from here that visitors can go for one-mile trolley and four-mile train rides.

The museum's collection includes 18 steam locomotives, 16 diesel locomotives, 6 electric locomotives, 38 passenger cars, 48 freight cars, 19 streetcars, 24 interurban cars, 20 rapid transit cars, 11 trolley buses, and a variety of steam and electric railroad work equipment. Among the features are the Burlington's *Nebraska Zephyr* and the North Shore Line's *Electroliner* trains.

The Burlington Railroad's Nebraska Zephyr.

The museum has streetcars that ran in Chicago, Milwaukee, St. Louis, Cleveland, and Philadelphia, as well as electric interurbans that operated on systems connecting Chicago to Milwaukee, South Bend, and the Fox River cities of Aurora, Geneva, St. Charles, and Elgin.

Examples of Chicago's transit history still operate at the museum. The only surviving CTA "Green Hornet" streetcar, for example, is used for rides. Wooden and steel elevated cars from Chicago's past also are on display.

MOTOROLA MUSEUM OF ELECTRONICS

Motorola, Inc.
1297 East Algonquin Road
Schaumburg, Illinois 60196
708/576-6559

Hours Monday–Friday, 9–5. Closed weekends.
Admission Free.

The Motorola Museum of Electronics was opened in 1991 by Motorola, Inc., a leading electronics manufacturer, on the grounds of its headquarters in Schaumburg. The 85,000-square-foot facility features historical, video, and interactive exhibits on major achievements in electronics and communications this century.

The museum has a 20,000-square-foot core exhibit space that is arranged thematically in two major sections. One section deals with current electronics technology and the other is devoted to the electronics industry as experienced by Motorola since its founding in 1928.

The current technology section offers exhibits on radio communications, microelectronics, automotive electronics, cellular telecommunications, electronic manufacturing techniques, engineering principles, and scientific concepts.

More than 500 artifacts are in the historical section—pertaining to early car and home radio from the 1930s, military and industrial communications from the 1940s, the golden age of television in the 1950s, the transistor revolution of the 1960s, and the integrated circuit and information age in the 1970s and 1980s.

One of the exhibits at the Museum of Broadcast Communications.

MUSEUM OF BROADCAST COMMUNICATIONS

800 South Wells Street
Chicago, Illinois 60607
312/987-1500

Hours Wednesday, Thursday, Friday, and Sunday, 12–5;
Saturday, 10–5. Closed Monday–Tuesday.
Admission Adults, $3; students, $2; senior citizens and children
under 13, $1.

Visitors can experience a couple of decades in an afternoon,
reliving the golden era of radio and television, at Chicago's
Museum of Broadcast Communications, one of only two
publicly accessible television and radio archives in the na-

tion. Its library contains 3,500 television programs, 49,000 radio shows, and 5,000 broadcast commercials.

In addition to the computer-catalogued archives, the museum offers a number of entertaining exhibits, including the popular "MBC Newscenter," at which you can make a tape of your own 15-minute "newscast" (available for purchase at $19.95). Other exhibits include: "The One-Minute Miracle," "The Story of Broadcast Advertising," "The Edgar Bergen and Charlie McCarthy Exhibit," "The Sportscaster's Cafe," "The Great Debate," "Garfield Goose and Friends," "The Fibber McGee and Molly Exhibit," "The Commercial Mini-Theatre," and more.

Live radio broadcasts originate from the museum each Saturday afternoon. There are ongoing screening exhibitions in the Kraft Television Theatre, such as "Rock 'n' Roll on Television," "Vietnam on Television—Television on Vietnam," "American Children's Television Festival," and "CNN: The First Ten Years." The museum also has a Commercial Break Gift Shop.

MUSEUM OF HOLOGRAPHY/CHICAGO

1134 West Washington Boulevard
Chicago, Illinois 60607
312/226-1007

Hours Wednesday–Sunday, 12:30–5; group tours by appointment. Closed Monday–Tuesday.
Admission Adults and children, $2.50; children under 6, free.

The Museum of Holography/Chicago was founded in 1976 to display holography to the general public and to encourage the advancement and development of the field through its teaching and research facilities. The holographic center is said to be the most complete institution of its type in the world.

Holography—the ability to produce images in full dimension, down to molecular exactness—promises to have far-reaching effects in almost every field of human endeavor, including medicine, engineering, architecture, and the arts.

A permanent collection of holograms is displayed at the museum, as well as changing exhibitions on the subject. Lectures and workshops also are available on different aspects of holography. Instruction in holography and allied fields (such as optics, photochemistry, interferometric holography, pulsed holography, and the physics of light) is given over 10 to 14 weeks with three fully equipped laboratories.

PRINTERS ROW PRINTING MUSEUM

715 South Plymouth Court
Chicago, Illinois 60605
312/987-1059

Hours Saturday, 9–5; Sunday, 10–4. Closed Monday–Friday, New Year's Day, Mother's Day, Memorial Day, Father's Day, and Christmas.
Admission Free.

An 1884 building in the Printers Row district on Chicago's South Side serves as the home for this historic printing museum. The Lakeside Press Building was occupied by the R.R. Donnelley Company from 1886 to 1925.

The collections include nineteenth-century printing presses and the Gordon Martin collection of eighteenth- and nineteenth-century posters, playbills, and assorted printed ephemera. The museum designs and prints wedding invitations, announcements, and Christmas cards on its 100-year-old printing presses.

SCIENCE AND TECHNOLOGY INTERACTIVE CENTER

18 West Benton Street
Aurora, Illinois 60506
708/859-3434

Hours Thursday, Friday, and Sunday, 12–5;
Saturday, 10–5. Closed Monday–Wednesday.
Admission Adults, $4; senior citizens, students and children
over 5, $2; families, $8.

One of the newest museums is the Science and Technology Interactive Center (better knows as SciTech), opened in 1990 in the former Post Office building in Aurora's downtown historical district. Before moving to Aurora, SciTech had a temporary home in Naperville for about a year.

More than 100 exhibits—most of them hands-on—demonstrate scientific principles of mathematics, chemistry, particle science, weather, magnetics, light and sound. The center also offers lectures and demonstrations on science.

"Molecules and Society," a traveling exhibition from the City of Science and Industry in Paris, was presented as the opening temporary exhibition. It traced the history of chemistry and the molding of molecules.

VOLO ANTIQUE AUTO MUSEUM AND VILLAGE

27582 West Highway 120
Volo, Illinois 60073
815/385-3644

Hours Daily, 10–5. Closed New Year's Day, Easter,
Thanksgiving, and Christmas.
Admission Adults, $2.50; senior citizens, $2; children 4–12,
$1.50. Special group rates.

One hundred antique and collector cars and exhibits can
be seen at this automobile museum. In addition to the autos,
the museum has a blacksmith shop, print shop, jail, filling
station, galleries, shops, and a restaurant.

OTHER MUSEUMS

Some museums do not fit into the traditional museum categories. They generally deal with fields not covered in typical museums.

The Chicago area has three such museums: the American Police Center and Museum, the Bradford Museum of Collector's Plates, and the Peace Museum. All tend to be small and highly focused in their specialties.

American Police Center and Museum.

AMERICAN POLICE CENTER AND MUSEUM

1717 South State Avenue
Chicago, Illinois 60616
312/431-0005

Hours Monday–Friday, 8:30–4:30; weekend tours
by appointment.
Admission Suggested donation—adults, $2; senior citizens,
$1.50; children 6–11, $1. Group rates—adults, $1; children, 50¢.

The primary objective of this museum is to improve understanding between police and the public in a cooperative
effort to reduce crime. Guided tours are offered of the exhibits that deal with the history and importance of law
enforcement, with an emphasis on police equipment.

Police artifacts, uniforms, weapons, documents, and
photographs pertaining to law enforcement are featured.
Other exhibits are aimed largely at younger visitors and
focus on traffic safety and drug abuse. In addition, the
museum has a theater where educational films on various
aspects of law enforcement are shown

Bradford Museum of Collector's Plates.

BRADFORD MUSEUM OF COLLECTOR'S PLATES

9333 Milwaukee Avenue
Niles, Illinois 60648
708/966-2770

Hours Monday–Friday, 9–4; Saturday–Sunday, 10–5. Guided
tours by appointment.
Admission Adults, $2; senior citizens, $1; children under 12,
free; tours, $1. Saturday, free

The world's largest permanent display of limited-edition
collector's plates can be seen at this corporate museum
operated by the Bradford Exchange. More than 1,000 porcelain, china, crystal, and wood plates produced by over 60
makers from 14 countries are shown, including the works of

Wedgwood, Royal Doulton, D'Arceau-Limoges, Rosenthal, Bing & Grondahl, Lalique, Haviland, Pickard, and Royal Copenhagen.

During business hours, visitors can observe brokers in action on the computerized trading floor with an electronic tote board that displays the latest market price for collector's plates. Indoor tropical gardens also can be seen at the Bradford Exchange headquarters.

The museum is temporarily closed to accommodate the expansion of the headquarters. It is expected to reopen in 1991, when the headquarters' new addition should be completed.

PEACE MUSEUM

430 West Erie Street
Chicago, Illinois 60610
312/440-1860

Hours Daily, 12–5; Thursday, 12–8.
Admission Adults, $3.50; students and senior citizens, $2.

The Peace Museum is the only museum in the nation presenting exhibitions regularly on issues of war and peace, as well as having collections and programs on the history of peacemaking. The small storefront museum has attracted wide attention for its work in the field.

Among the offerings have been an exhibition on Dr. Martin Luther King, Jr.'s peacemaker role and alternatives to war-like toys for children. Nearly half of the museum's exhibitions have become traveling exhibits, with a number containing resource materials pertaining to the topics.

COMMERCIAL ART GALLERIES

The Chicago area has a wide range of commercial galleries that cover almost every form of art—many with specialties. Most are located on Chicago's Near North Side, but galleries also can be found in some neighborhoods and the suburbs.

Abel Joseph Gallery
1600 North Milwaukee Avenue
Chicago, Illinois 60647
312/384-4959

Contemporary artworks.

Robert Henry Adams Gallery
1480 West Webster Street
Chicago, Illinois 60614
312/327-6542

American paintings and prints of the twentieth century.

Jean Albano Gallery
311 West Superior Street
Chicago, Illinois 60610
312/440-0770

West Coast and contemporary American artists.

Galerie Americana
320 West Illinois Street
Chicago, Illinois 60610
312/337-2670

American, Latin American, Caribbean, and African-American art.

American West
2110 North Halsted Street
Chicago, Illinois 60614
312/871-0400

Fine Southwest art and Native American artifacts.

Ancient Echoes
1800 North Clybourn Avenue
Chicago, Illinois 60614
312/337-7733

Contemporary jewelry and fine art inspired by ancient and ethnic images.

Animation Plus!
790 North Milwaukee Avenue
Chicago, Illinois 60622
312/243-8666

Original and limited edition animation art, drawings, and celluloids.

Ariel Gallery
15 West Jefferson Avenue
Naperville, Illinois 60540
708/355-4466

Contemporary crafts and fine art, including works in fiber, clay, glass, wood, and metal; jewelry; wearables; sculpture; watercolors; and prints.

Artisan Shop and Gallery
Plaza del Lago
1515 Sheridan Road
Wilmette, Illinois 60091
708/251-3775

American crafts, including ceramics, jewelry, wearable art, weavings, glass, and wood.

Artisans 21
5225 South Harper Avenue
Chicago, Illinois 60615
312/288-7450

Photography, soft sculpture, papier mâché, stained glass, ceramics, painting, jewelry, hand weaving, and wearable art.

Austin Galleries
677 North Michigan Avenue
Chicago, Illinois 60610
312/943-3730

Woodfield Mall, Main Level
Schaumburg, Illinois 60194
708/882-0030

Finley Square Mall
Downers Grove, Illinois 60515
708/629-1177

Traditional and contemporary works of art.

Authurian Gallery
5962 North Elston Avenue
Chicago, Illinois 60646
312/775-5007

Oils, watercolors, and bronzes by nearly 50 participating artists.

Jacques Baruch Gallery
40 East Delaware Place
Chicago, Illinois 60611
312/955-3377

Eastern European art.

Mary Bell Gallery
215 West Superior Street
Chicago, Illinois 60610
312/642-0202

Contemporary Pan-American paintings, sculpture, and works on paper.

Benjamin-Beattie Ltd.
1000 Lake Shore Drive
Chicago, Illinois 60611
312/337-1343

Contemporary master graphics, American regional art, prints, and multimedia sculpture.

Walter Bischoff Gallery
340 West Huron Street, Third Floor
Chicago, Illinois 60610
312/266-0244

Contemporary paintings, works on paper, and recent European art.

Roy Boyd Gallery
739 North Wells Street
Chicago, Illinois 60610
312/642-1606

Contemporary American abstract paintings and sculpture.

Brandywine Fantasy Gallery
750 North Orleans Street
Chicago, Illinois 60610
312/951-8466

Fine American paintings, featuring Brandywine tradition and American fantasy art.

Rita Bucheit Gallery
500 North Wells Street
Chicago, Illinois 60610
312/527-4080

European furniture and fine arts, specializing in Biedermeir and Empire.

Campanile-Capponi Ltd.
1252 North State Parkway
Chicago, Illinois 60610
312/642-3869

Contemporary Midwestern art—wall hangings, sculpture, pottery, paintings, and mixed media.

Campanile Galleries Inc.
200 South Michigan Avenue
Chicago, Illinois 60604
312/663-3885

Nineteenth- and early twentieth-century American and European masters.

Casa Del Rio Gallery
341 West Superior Street
Chicago, Illinois 60610
312/751-1961

Specializing in antique ethnographic textiles.

CCA Gallery
325 West Huron Street
Chicago, Illinois 60610
312/944-0094

Contemporary paintings, sculpture, prints, and works on paper.

Centurion Galleries
540 North Michigan Avenue, Suite 112-A
Chicago, Illinois 60611
312/661-0220

Nineteenth- and twentieth-century paintings, drawings, and master graphics by European and American artists.

Merrill Chase Galleries
Water Tower Place, Second Level
835 North Michigan Avenue
Chicago, Illinois 60611
312/337-6600

Woodfield Shopping Center
Schaumburg, Illinois 60172
708/330-0300

172 Oakbrook Center
Oak Brook, Illinois 60521
708/572-0225

Paintings, graphics, sculpture, and tapestries by the masters and contemporary artists.

Chiaroscuro Gallery
750 North Orleans Street
Chicago, Illinois 60610
312/988-9253

Contemporary fine art and crafts.

Chicago Art Network
118 North Peoria Street
Chicago, Illinois 60607
312/829-3915

Contemporary works by Chicago-area artists.

Chicago Center for the Print Ltd.
1509 West Fullerton Avenue
Chicago, Illinois 60614
312/477-1585

Original prints in a wide range of techniques by artists of Chicago and the Midwest.

Jan Cicero Gallery
221 West Erie Street
Chicago, Illinois 60610
312/440-1904

Contemporary art with regional emphasis.

Circle Studio
5600 North Western Avenue
Chicago, Illinois 60659
312/275-5454

Stained glass creations.

Eva Cohon Gallery Ltd.
301 West Superior Street
Chicago, Illinois 60610
312/664-3669

2057 Green Bay Road
Highland Park, Illinois 60035
708/432-7310

Contemporary American paintings, sculpture, and works on paper.

Collectable Arts Inc.
1961 North Halsted Street
Chicago, Illinois 60614
312/944-1447

Hand-crafted items, including hand-blown glass, Oriental rugs, textiles, wall hangings, and copper and brass works.

CompassRose Gallery
325 West Huron Street
Chicago, Illinois 60610
312/266-0434

Modern and contemporary art.

Corporate Art Source Inc.
900 North Franklin Street
Chicago, Illinois 60610
312/751-1300

Contemporary art.

Cortland-Leyten Gallery
213 North Morgan Street
Chicago, Illinois 60607
312/733-2781

Ethnographic and folk arts of the Americas.

Creative Claythings
3412 North Southport Avenue
Chicago, Illinois 60657
312/472-5580

Ceramic artworks by Illinois and Mexican artists, as well as imported handcrafts.

Cross Currents
1446 West Irving Park Road
Chicago, Illinois 60613
312/880-5780

Contemporary artwork with Southwestern highlights.

Dart Gallery
750 North Orleans Street
Chicago, Illinois 60610
312/787-6366

Contemporary American paintings and sculpture.

Douglas Dawson Gallery
814 North Franklin Street
Chicago, Illinois 60610
312/751-1961

Ancient and historic textiles.

De Graaf Fine Art Inc.
9 East Superior Street
Chicago, Illinois 60611
312/951-5180

Works of American, Latin American, and European contemporary artists.

Deson-Saunders Gallery
750 North Orleans Street
Chicago, Illinois 60610
312/787-0005

Twentieth-century contemporary American and European art.

Detrick-Artes Gallery
213 North Morgan Street
Chicago, Illinois 60607
312/829-7749

Imported art, antiques, and furniture from Thailand, Mexico, Spain, Africa, and Haiti.

East West Contemporary Art
311 West Superior Street
Chicago, Illinois 60610
312/664-8003

Contemporary artworks by Chinese and international artists.

Catherine Edelman Gallery
300 West Superior Street
Chicago, Illinois 60610
312/266-2350

Photography.

Ehlers-Caudill Gallery
750 North Orleans Street
Chicago, Illinois 60610
312/642-9611

Master photographs from twentieth-century and contemporary photo-based artworks.

1800 Clybourn Galleries
1800 North Clybourn Avenue
Chicago, Illinois 60614
312/951-1855

Rotating exhibitions.

Erie Street Gallery
400 West Erie Street
Chicago, Illinois 60610
312/266-7872

Contemporary American art.

Fairweather Hardin Gallery
101 East Ontario Street
Chicago, Illinois 60611
312/642-0007

Contemporary art by American and European artists.

Feigen Inc.
325 West Huron Street
Chicago, Illinois 60610
312/787-0500

Contemporary art and old masters.

Walter Findlay Galleries Inc.
814 North Michigan Avenue
Chicago, Illinois 60611
312/649-1500

Twentieth-century French masters and contemporary American and European artists.

Fly-by-Nite Gallery
714 North Wells Street
Chicago, Illinois 60610
312/664-8136

Pre-Raphaelite art, art nouveau, American and European art and crafts, art deco, secession art, modern art, pottery, bronzes, paintings, graphics, posters, advertising art, and paper ephemera and philatelic items.

Oskar Friedl Gallery
750 North Orleans Street
Chicago, Illinois 60610
312/337-7550

Contemporary American and European art.

Funhouse Gallery
1139 West Fulton Market
Chicago, Illinois 60607
312/226-4255

Pop and contemporary works in all media.

Gallery 58
18 East Huron Street
Chicago, Illinois 60611
312/787-5066

Contemporary Polish art.

Kay Garvey Gallery
230 West Superior Street
Chicago, Illinois 60610
312/440-0522

Constructions, sculpture, and textiles.

GeorgeArt
1549 North Wells Street
Chicago, Illinois 60610
312/751-9277

Devoted entirely to the work of George Colin.

Gilman/Gruen Galleries
226 West Superior Street
Chicago, Illinois 60610
312/337-6262

Contemporary painting, drawing, and sculpture, as well as African, Haitian, and Oceanic art.

Goldman-Kraft Gallery
301 West Superior Street
Chicago, Illinois 60610
312/943-9088

Contemporary art in all media by American, European, and Israeli artists.

Grove Street Gallery-Studio
919 Grove Street
Evanston, Illinois 60201
312/866-7340

Contemporary, traditional, and naive paintings, graphics, sculpture, and stained glass.

Richard Gray Gallery
620 North Michigan Avenue
Chicago, Illinois 60611
312/642-8877

Contemporary and modern-master paintings, sculpture, drawings, and prints.

Hamlet Gallery Ltd.
1412 North Wells Street
Chicago, Illinois 60610
312/642-4444

Modern and contemporary paintings, sculpture, and works on paper, with emphasis on developing and emerging artists.

Carl Hammer Gallery
200 West Superior Street
Chicago, Illinois 60610
312/266-8512

Historical and contemporary art emphasizing the work of self-taught and outsider artists.

Carl Hammer Gallery/Riverside
415 North Sangamon Street
Chicago, Illinois 60622
312/421-3600

Experimental showspace for emerging and large-scale installations.

Hildt Galleries
6 West Hubbard Street
Chicago, Illinois 60610
312/527-3525
Fine nineteenth- and twentieth-century paintings.

Rhona Hoffman Gallery
215 West Superior Street
Chicago, Illinois 60610
312/951-8828

American and European contemporary art.

Hokin Kaufman Gallery
210 West Superior Street
Chicago, Illinois 60610
312/266-1211

Contemporary paintings, sculpture and artist-designed furniture.

Joy Horwich Gallery
226 East Ontario Street
Chicago, Illinois 60611
312/787-0171

Contemporary paintings, sculpture, silk wall hangings, and picture quilts by artists who have emerged.

Edwynn Houk Gallery
200 West Superior Street
Chicago, Illinois 60610
312/943-0698

Twentieth-century photographs.

Insam/Gleicher Gallery
750 North Orleans Street
Chicago, Illinois 60610
312/951-5419

Contemporary art.

Gwenda Jay Gallery
301 West Superior Street
Chicago, Illinois 60610
312/664-3406

Contemporary paintings, drawings, and sculpture.

R. S. Johnson Fine Art
645 North Michigan Avenue
Chicago, Illinois 60611
312/943-1661

Nineteenth- and twentieth-century master paintings, drawings, graphics, and sculpture, and old master and modern prints and drawings from 1475 to the present.

Rodi Karkazis Gallery
168 North Michigan Avenue, Suite 300
Chicago, Illinois 60601
312/346-5050

European antique oils and watercolors and twentieth-century Chinese art, including works by Capron, Zouni, Fassianos, Ting, and others.

Kass/Meridian Gallery
215 West Superior Street, Second Floor
Chicago, Illinois 60610
312/266-5999

Master contemporary prints.

Douglas Kenyon Inc.
1357 North Wells Street
Chicago, Illinois 60610
312/642-5300

The art of John James Audubon and similar artists.

Phyllis Kind Gallery
313 West Superior Street
Chicago, Illinois 60610
312/642-6302

Contemporary American and Soviet art.

Kirmse's Limited Editions
128 West Lake Street
Bloomingdale, Illinois 60108
708/894-0594

Wall art from originals, limited editions, prints, and posters, as well as glass, pottery, porcelain, sandcasting, portraits, and custom jewelry.

Klein Art Works
400 North Morgan Street
Chicago, Illinois 60622
312/243-0400

Abstract paintings and sculpture by emerging and established American and international artists.

Laguna Gallery
301 West Superior Street
Chicago, Illinois 60610
312/751-2522

Oil paintings, serigraphs, and lithographs.

Landfall Press Gallery
311 West Superior Street
Chicago, Illinois 60610
312/787-2578

Contemporary lithographs, woodcuts, and etchings.

Lannon Gallery
119 North Peoria Street, Suite 3C
Chicago, Illinois 60607
312/829-4541

Contemporary emerging artists.

Les Primitifs
706 North Wells Street
Chicago, Illinois 60610
312/787-9440

Traditional and contemporary art from Africa, New Guinea, and Southeast Asia.

Lightwriters Neon Gallery
911 Green Bay Road
Winnetka, Illinois 60093
708/441-6090

Artworks in neon, mixed media, and handblown glass.

Lincoln Gallery
3039 North Lincoln Avenue
Chicago, Illinois 60657
312/248-3647
Nineteenth and early twentieth-century paintings and graphics.

Robbin Lockett Gallery
703 North Wells Street
Chicago, Illinois 60610
312/649-1230

Contemporary art.

R. H. Love Galleries
100 East Ohio Street
Chicago, Illinois 60611
312/664-9620

American masters of the eighteenth and nineteenth centuries, a twentieth-century gallery, and folk art galleries.

Nancy Lurie Gallery
1632 North LaSalle Street
Chicago, Illinois 60614
312/337-2883

Contemporary American art.

Lydon Fine Art Inc.
203 West Superior Street
Chicago, Illinois 60610
312/943-1133

Contemporary European and American art.

Mars Gallery
1139 West Fulton Market
Chicago, Illinois 60607
312/226-7808

Pop and outsider works in all media.

Marx Gallery
208 West Kinzie Street
Chicago, Illinois 60610
312/464-0400

Contemporary studio glass art, sculpture, and painting.

Masterworks Gallery
1874 Sheridan Road
Highland Park, Illinois 60035
708/432-2787

Contemporary craft artists working in metal, wood, and mixed media.

Millburn Gallery
38500 Route 45
Millburn, Illinois 60083
708/356-3022

Works by regional artists.

Peter Miller Gallery
401 West Superior Street
Chicago, Illinois 60610
312/951-0252
Contemporary painting, sculpture, and photography of American artists.

Mindscape Gallery
1506 Sherman Avenue
Evanston, Illinois 60201
312/864-2660

Crafts and art by contemporary American artists.

Galerie Thomas R. Monahan
1038 North LaSalle Street
Chicago, Illinois 60610
312/266-7530

Modern and contemporary paintings, drawings, and sculpture.

Mongerson-Wunderlich Gallery
704 North Wells Street
Chicago, Illinois 60610
312/943-2354

Nineteenth- and twentieth-century American artists.

R. A. Nantus Gallery
2355 North Clark Street
Chicago, Illinois 60614
312/248-6660

Contemporary and antique prints from the U.S., Europe, and Far East.

Isobel Neal Gallery
200 West Superior Street
Chicago, Illinois 60610
312/944-1570

Works by African-American artists.

Neville-Sargent Gallery
708 North Wells Street and 311 West Superior Street
Chicago, Illinois 60610
312/664-2787

Contemporary American and international paintings, sculpture, drawings, prints, and fiber works.

Nicole Gallery
734 North Wells Street
Chicago, Illinois 60610
312/787-7716

Paintings, sculpture, wood carvings, and crafts from Haiti.

1935 Gallery
1935 South Halsted Street
Chicago, Illinois 60608
312/829-0485

Emerging artists.

Objects Gallery
230 West Huron Street
Chicago, Illinois 60610
312/664-6622

Contemporary art and artist-designed furniture.

Orca Aart
300 West Grand Avenue
Chicago, Illinois 60610
312/245-5245

Art from the Arctic, Africa, and the Pacific Northwest.

Out of the West
2187 North Clybourn Avenue
Chicago, Illinois 60614
312/404-9278

Handcrafted silver jewelry and wearable art and home accessories by Native American and Western artists.

Nina Owen Ltd.
212 West Superior Street
Chicago, Illinois 60610
312/664-0474

Specializing in contemporary sculpture.

Pas de chat
3542 North Southport Street
Chicago, Illinois 60657
312/871-2818

Fine crafts and art in glass, wood, metal, fiber, ceramics, and fine jewelry.

Perimeter Gallery
750 North Orleans Street
Chicago, Illinois 60610
312/266-9473

Contemporary painting, works on paper, sculpture, and crafts by emerging artists.

Maya Polsky Gallery
311 West Superior Street
Chicago, Illinois 60610
312/440-0055
Contemporary Soviet paintings and drawings.

Portals Ltd.
230 West Huron Street
Chicago, Illinois 60610
312/642-1066

Naif paintings in room settings.

Poster Plus, Inc.
210 South Michigan Avenue
Chicago, Illinois 60604
312/461-9277

2906 North Broadway Avenue
Chicago, Illinois 60657
312/549-2822

Contemporary posters of museum exhibits, Chicago cultural events, and vintage originals.

Prince Galleries
357 West Erie Street
Chicago, Illinois 60610
312/266-9663

Realistic paintings and sculpture by contemporary Chicago artists.

Printworks Ltd.
311 West Superior Street
Chicago, Illinois 60610
312/664-9407

Contemporary prints, drawings, photographs, and artists' books.

Kenneth Probst Galleries
620 North Michigan Avenue
Chicago, Illinois 60611
312/440-1990

American and European Impressionism.

Roger Ramsay Gallery
212 West Superior Street, Suite 503
Chicago, Illinois 60610
312/337-4678

Contemporary American and European paintings, drawings, and sculpture.

Ratner Gallery
750 North Orleans Street
Chicago, Illinois 60610
312/944-8884

American and European modern and contemporary paintings, sculpture, and works on paper.

Galleria Renata
507 North Wells Street
Chicago, Illinois 60610
312/644-1607

Contemporary paintings and sculpture by international and emerging artists.

Ricky Renier Gallery
1550 North Milwaukee Avenue
Chicago, Illinois 60622
312/227-3090

Contemporary American and European art.

Rezac Gallery
212 West Superior Street
Chicago, Illinois 60610
312/751-0481

Contemporary decorative and fine arts, specializing in modern jewelry.

Betsy Rosenfield Gallery
212 West Superior Street
Chicago, Illinois 60610
312/787-8020

Contemporary paintings, sculpture, photography, and studio glass.

J. Rosenthal Fine Arts Ltd.
230 West Superior Street
Chicago, Illinois 60610
312/642-2966

Modern and contemporary paintings, sculpture, and works on paper.

Esther Saks Gallery
311 West Superior Street
Chicago, Illinois 60610
312/751-0911

Contemporary ceramic sculpture, paintings, mixed media, and works on paper by emerging and established artists.

Sazama Gallery
300 West Superior Street
Chicago, Illinois 60610
312/951-0004

Contemporary American art.

Schneider-Blum-Loeb Gallery Inc.
230 West Superior Street
Chicago, Illinois 60610
312/988-4033

Ceramics and jewelry.

Stephen Solovy Fine Art
620 North Michigan Avenue
Chicago, Illinois 60611
312/664-4860

American and European modern and contemporary paintings, drawings, and sculpture, and prints.

Southwest Expressions
1459 West Webster Street
Chicago, Illinois 60614
312/525-2626

Contemporary native American and Southwestern paintings, furniture, sculpture, pottery, weavings, and jewelry.

Samuel Stein Fine Arts Ltd.
620 North Michigan Avenue, Suite 340
Chicago, Illinois 60611
312/337-1782

Nineteenth- and twentieth-century paintings, graphics, and sculpture.

Galleries Maurice Sternberg
Drake Hotel Arcade
North Michigan Avenue at Walton Street
Chicago, Illinois 60611
312/642-1700

Nineteenth- and twentieth-century American and European paintings and drawings.

Struve Gallery
309 West Superior Street
Chicago, Illinois 60610
312/787-0563

Contemporary American and Soviet art and decorative arts.

van Straaten Gallery
230 West Huron Street and 742 North Wells Street
Chicago, Illinois 60610
312/642-2900

Contemporary master prints.

Gallery Venzor
301 West Superior Street
Chicago, Illinois 60610
312/642-8122

Latin American and European contemporary and emerging artists.

Gallery Vienna
750 North Orleans Street
Chicago, Illinois 60610
312/951-0300

Austrian furniture and objects of art.

Mario Villa Gallery
500 North Wells Street
Chicago, Illinois 60610
312/923-0993

Steel, brass, and bronze furniture, sculpture, and paintings.

Ruth Volid Gallery Ltd.
225 West Illinois Street
Chicago, Illinois 60610
312/644-3180

Traditional and contemporary art in all media.

Waller-Boldenweck Gallery
5300 South Blackstone Avenue
Chicago, Illinois 60615
312/363-7446

Realism to abstract, original paintings to graphics, and limited edition prints and posters.

Walton Street Gallery
58 East Walton Street
Chicago, Illinois 60610
312/943-1793

Traditional and contemporary art.

Wickers Gallery
1564 North Milwaukee Avenue
Chicago, Illinois 60622
312/486-5977

American and European oils, from the traditional to high tech.

Wild Goose Chase Quilt Gallery
6977 North Sheridan Road
Chicago, Illinois 60626
312/465-8787

903 Sheridan Avenue
Evanston, Illinois 60202
708/328-1808

American quilts, circa 1840 to modern.

Wade Wilson Gallery
750 North Orleans Street
Chicago, Illinois 60610
312/440-9010

Contemporary paintings, sculpture, and works on paper.

Worthington Gallery
620 North Michigan Avenue
Chicago, Illinois 60611
312/266-2424

German art of the twentieth century from the expressionists
to contemporary art, as well as master paintings, drawings,
sculpture, and graphics.

Yolanda Gallery
300 West Superior Street
Chicago, Illinois 60610
312/664-3436

Twentieth-century American, European, and Asian native,
folk, and outsider art.

Donald Young Gallery
325 West Huron Street
Chicago, Illinois 60610
312/664-2151

Contemporary art and sculpture.

Zaks Gallery
620 North Michigan Avenue
Chicago, Illinois 60611
312/943-8440

Contemporary paintings, drawings, and sculpture—interior
and large-scale sculpture for public places.

Zolla/Lieberman Gallery
230 West Huron Street
Chicago, Illinois 60610
312/944-1990

Contemporary paintings and sculpture.

NOT-FOR-PROFIT GALLERIES AND COLLECTIVES

In addition to the art galleries listed elsewhere, Chicago has a number of not-for-profit galleries and collectives featuring the works of emerging and established artists from Chicago and elsewhere. Among these facilities are the following:

A.R.C. Gallery
1040 West Huron Street
Chicago, Illinois 60622
312/733-2787

Contemporary and innovative artworks.

Artemisia Gallery
700 North Carpenter Street
Chicago, Illinois 60622
312/226-7323

Contemporary gallery operated by a women's group.

Arts Club of Chicago
109 East Ontario Street
Chicago, Illinois 60610
312/787-3997

A collection of works by masters and contemporary artists, as well as changing exhibitions.

Beacon Street Gallery
4520 North Beacon Street
Chicago, Illinois 60640
312/561-3500

Contemporary art.

Contemporary Art Workshop
542 West Grant Place
Chicago, Illinois 60614
312/472-4004

Works by emerging artists in all media.

N.A.M.E.
700 North Carpenter Street
Chicago, Illinois 60622
312/226-0671

Contemporary artworks.

North River Community Gallery
3307 West Bryn Mawr
Chicago, Illinois 60659
312/583-4050

Community art gallery.

Prairie Avenue Gallery
1900 South Prairie Avenue
Chicago, Illinois 60616
312/842-4523

Changing exhibitions.

Randolph Gallery
756 North Milwaukee Avenue
Chicago, Illinois 60622
312/666-7737

Contemporary, innovative, and experimental art in different media and community-based public projects.

School of the Art Institute of Chicago Gallery 2
1040 West Huron Street
Chicago, Illinois 60622
312/226-4449

Art works by students at the Art Institute School.

Textile Arts Centre
916 West Diversey Parkway
Chicago, Illinois 60614
312/929-5655

Fiber work by contemporary artists and textiles.

Upstart Gallery
1712 North Halsted Street
Chicago, Illinois 60614
312/266-1230

Chicago-area artists.

CORPORATE ART COLLECTIONS

Approximately 50 Chicago-area companies have extensive corporate art collections, but only about half are open to the public. The works of art are used primarily to decorate office and hall areas, although some firms have public galleries and lobby displays. Among the companies that permit public visitations (and sometimes will arrange tours for groups) are:

Amalgamated Trust & Savings Bank
1 West Monroe Street
Chicago, Illinois 60690
312/822-3180

Nineteenth- and twentieth-century graphics, oils, tapestries, drawings, sculpture, and collages in the main bank.

Amoco Corporation
200 East Randolph Drive
Chicago, Illinois 60601
312/856-7165

Primarily contemporary graphics, this collection consists of 6,500 original artworks by 1,800 artists from 81 countries, including 1,300 pieces by almost 400 artists from the Chicago area. Only works in public areas are available for viewing.

Borg-Warner Corporation
200 South Michigan Avenue
Chicago, Illinois 60604
312/322-8653

A collection of over 500 artworks by Chicago and regional artists. Media include paintings, prints, sculpture, and photographs, drawings, fiber works, ceramics, glass, and constructions. Not usually accessible for public viewing, but sometimes advance arrangements can be made for special small groups.

Cole Taylor Bank/Main
1965 North Milwaukee Avenue
Chicago, Illinois 60647
312/278-6800

Imagist art and works by related groups of the 1970s are in this collection located throughout the bank in public areas and executive offices.

Cole Taylor Financial Group Inc.
350 East Dundee Road
Wheeling, Illinois 60090
708/459-1111

Contemporary and southwestern artworks are located throughout the company's office area.

Continental Bank
231 South LaSalle Street
Chicago, Illinois 60697
312/923-6902

A general collection of 6,000 artworks consisting primarily of drawings, paintings, sculpture, and original limited-edition prints. Viewing requests considered on an individual basis.

First National Bank of Chicago
1 First National Plaza
Chicago, Illinois 60670
312/732-5935

More than 4,100 paintings, drawings, sculptures, tapestries, and graphics from the sixth century B.C. to the present located throughout the Chicago headquarters, regional offices, and overseas offices. Limited tours (restricted to 20 people) are available by appointment at the headquarters building.

Harris Trust & Savings Bank
111 West Monroe Street
Chicago, Illinois 60603
312/461-2121

A collection of tapestries, sculpture, and paintings can be seen.

Illinois Bell Telephone Company
225 West Randolph Street
Chicago, Illinois 60606
312/727-9411

Illinois Bell has a collection of approximately 900 works of contemporary art, with an emphasis on Illinois artists. But the permanent collection is located in private office areas and not open to the public. However, changing art exhibitions are presented in a lobby gallery.

Kemper Group National Insurance Companies
Long Grove, Illinois 60049
708/540-2502

A collection of 675 works of contemporary American art, with the emphasis on artists of Chicago and the Midwest. Works are rotated throughout the halls and working areas. Tours are available to nonprofit groups of 5 to 25 by advance reservation with the curator.

LaSalle National Bank
120 South LaSalle Street
Chicago, Illinois 60603
312/443-2000

A historical collection of about 2,000 works, including important photographs and photographers from the earliest recorded images to the present. Located in public areas of the bank.

McDonald's Corporation
1 McDonald's Plaza
Oak Brook, Illinois 60521
708/887-3585

This collection of 300 works, primarily of contemporary art, includes paintings, sculpture, graphics, and fiber work at the corporate headquarters and training center as well as regional and international offices. Tours must be arranged in advance.

Old Kent Bank of Chicago
Sears Tower
Chicago, Illinois 60606
312/876-4200

A collection of contemporary American art from 1960 to the present, with about 750 of the 125 works consisting of prints. The pieces are rotated through public spaces in the bank.

Playboy Enterprises, Inc.
680 North Lake Shore Drive
Chicago, Illinois 60611
312/751-8000

Original art commissioned for *Playboy* magazine and other works are part of this collection of nearly 4,000 pieces. Among the artists represented are Tom Wesselman, Roger Brown, Ed Paschke, Alfred Leslie, Alberto Vargas, and Andy Warhol. Sculptures by George Segal, Frank Gallo, and Richard Hunt also are on display. The works can be viewed by small groups upon appointment.

Sears, Roebuck & Company
Sears Tower
Chicago, Illinois 60684
312/875-2500

Sears' collection of some 8,000 works was originally started under the guidance of actor/collector Vincent Price. Among the artists represented are Henri Matisse, Georges Braque, Pablo Picasso, and Alexander Calder. But only Calder's monumental "Universe" sculpture in the lobby is available for public viewing.

MAJOR PUBLIC SCULPTURE

Chicago has become known for its large-scale sculpture in public places. Most of the best-known examples can be seen in the Loop central business area, but outstanding sculpture also can be found in Chicago's parks and the suburbs. Here are some representative major works:

LOOP AND CENTRAL BUSINESS AREA

Batcolumn by Claes Oldenberg
1977
Social Security Administration Building Plaza
600 West Madison Street

A 100-foot steel sculpture painted gray and shaped like a baseball bat.

Being Born by Virginio Ferrari
1982
State Street Mall
State and Washington streets

Made of stainless steel, this tribute to precise die making consists of two 20-foot circular elements set within a black marble reflecting pool.

Ceres by John Storrs
1930
Board of Trade Building
141 West Jackson Boulevard at LaSalle Street

This 30-foot-high statue of Ceres, the Roman goddess of grain, who was regarded as the patroness of corn traders, can be seen atop the pyramidal roof of the 45-story building that houses the world's busiest grain exchange.

Chicago Picasso by Pablo Picasso
1967
Richard J. Daley Civic Center Plaza
Washington and Dearborn streets

Known as "the Picasso," this 50-foot steel sculpture is of three-dimensional planar design abstracted from the head of a woman.

Dawn Shadows by Louise Nevelson
1983
Madison Plaza Building Plaza
Madison and Wells streets

A 30-foot steel painted black sculpture.

Defense, Regeneration, The Pioneers, The Discoverers by Henry Hering and James Earle Fraser
1928
Pylons at the Michigan Avenue Bridge
Michigan Avenue and the Chicago River

These four reliefs commemorate early events in the history of Chicago and are located near the sites of Fort Dearborn and the first permanent homestead in the area.

Flamingo by Alexander Calder
1974
Federal Center Plaza
Adams and Dearborn streets

A 53-foot painted steel abstract stabile.

The Four Seasons by Marc Chagall
1974
First National Plaza Monroe and Dearborn streets

A 70-by-14-by-10-foot mosaic of handchipped stone and glass fragments.

George Washington–Robert Morris–Haym Salomon Memorial Monument by Lorado Taft
1941
Heald Square
Wacker Drive and Wabash Avenue

This 11-foot bronze sculpture is known as the "Heald Square Monument."

Merchandise Mart Hall of Fame by Minna Harkavy, Milton Horn, Lewis Iselin, Henry Rox, and Charles Umlauf
1953
Main entrance to Merchandise Mart
Chicago River between Wells and Orleans streets

These eight bronze busts of leading American merchants—four times life-size and mounted on tall marble pillars outside the Mart—pay tribute to "the nation's geniuses of distribution."

Miro's Chicago by Joan Miro
1981
Brunswick Building Plaza
69 West Washington Street

A 39-foot figure made of steel, wire mesh, concrete, bronze, and ceramic tiles.

Monument with Standing Beast by Jean Dubuffet
1984
State of Illinois Building Plaza
Randolph and Clark streets

A 29-foot fiberglass abstract sculpture.

Sounding Sculpture by Harry Bertoia
1975
Amoco Building Plaza
200 East Randolph Street

A vibrating copper-beryllium, brass, and granite sounding sculpture fountain.

PARKS AND NEIGHBORHOODS

Abraham Lincoln by Augustus Saint-Gaudens
1887
East of the Chicago Historical Society
North Avenue near Clark Street, Lincoln Park

This 11½-foot standing figure of Abraham Lincoln, with his head bowed and his left hand clutching his coat's lapel, is considered to be Saint-Gaudens' masterpiece. He also did the seated sculpture of Lincoln in Grant Park.

Bison **by Edward Kemeys**
1893 (installed 1911)
Near Sacramento Boulevard and Division Street
Humboldt Park

These two bronze versions of American buffaloes, which face the sunken garden in Humboldt Park, were reproduced from models created by Kemeys for the 1893 World's Columbian Exposition.

Chicago Stock Exchange Arch **by Denkmar Adler and Louis Sullivan**
1893 (reinstalled at present location 1977)
East entrance of the Art Institute of Chicago
Columbus Drive at Monroe Street, Grant Park

This terra-cotta arch brace with a limestone backing was the dramatic entrance to the Chicago Stock Exchange for 80 years. Relocated and restored when the exchange building was demolished, it now is part of a pool-and-garden complex adjacent to the east entrance to the Art Institute.

Clarence Buckingham Fountain **by Bennett, Parsons & Frost in collaboration with Jacques H. Lambert, engineer, and Marcel Francois Loyau, artist-sculptor**
1927
At the foot of Congress Parkway
Grant Park

The world's largest decorative fountain at the time of its dedication, the fountain consists of three circular basins of Georgia pink marble carved in the beaux arts manner and decorated with shells, sea horses, and other sea motifs.

Elks National Memorial Sculpture **by Gerome Brush, Laura Gardin Fraser, and Adolph Alexander Weinman**
1926 (rededicated in 1946)
Elks National Memorial and Headquarters Building
2750 North Lakeview Avenue

A number of works of art—including two life-size bronze figures at the entrance, a 5-foot-high, 168-foot-long frieze, and two 14-foot-high sculptural groups—are part of this memorial to members of the Benevolent and Protective Order of Elks who died in World Wars I and II.

The Eugene Field Memorial **by Edward McCartan**
1922
East of the Small Animal House at Lincoln Park Zoo
Lincoln Park

A memorial to the noted poet in which a winged woman drops her flowers on two sleeping children against a background of reliefs illustrating some of Field's poems.

The Fountain of the Great Lakes **by Lorado Taft**
1913
South wing of the Art Institute of Chicago
Grant Park

Five female figures representing the five Great Lakes are grouped together so that water flows from shells they hold in the same way water passes through the lake system.

Fountain of Time by Lorado Taft
1922
West end of Midway Plaisance
Washington Park

"Time" stands as the lone sentinel across a pool of water from a 110-foot-long wave of humanity with 100 figures, cast in concrete.

From Here to There by Richard Hunt
1975
Martin Luther King Community Service Center
43rd Street and Cottage Grove Avenue

Two 7-foot-high bronze elements—one at the entrance and another in an open plaza 30 feet away—that are to be viewed as a single work of art.

General John Logan Memorial by Augustus Saint-Gaudens and Alexander Phimister Proctor
1897
Michigan Avenue at 9th Street
Grant Park

The Illinois-born Civil War general sits on his horse holding a flag picked up from a fallen color-bearer in this memorial.

I Will by Ellsworth Kelly
1981
Fullerton Avenue and Cannon Drive
Lincoln Park

A 40-foot-tall rectangular stainless steel column, from 5 to 6 feet wide with a 3-inch hollow center, that both reflects and distorts what is around it.

Illinois Centennial Memorial Column by Evelyn Beatrice Longman and Henry Bacon
1918
Logan Square
Logan Boulevard and Milwaukee Avenue

This Doric-style column commemorating the centenary of the admission of Illinois as a state is topped by a large eagle with spread wings and has numerous relief figures on the drum of the column.

In Celebration of the 200th Anniversary of the Founding of the Republic by Isamu Noguchi
1976
East facade of the Art Institute of Chicago
Columbus Drive between Monroe Street and Jackson Boulevard
Grant Park

Granite and stainless steel fountain.

Independence Square Fountain by Charles J. Mulligan
1902
Independence Square
Douglas and Independence boulevards

This once-grand fountain, also known as "The Fourth of July Fountain," has a 15-foot granite pedestal shaped like a bell topped by four bronze figures of children celebrating Independence Day.

Indians by Ivan Mestrovic
1928
Michigan Avenue at Congress Parkway
Grant Park

Two powerful Indian warriors riding huge horses provide a dramatic frame for Buckingham Fountain from Michigan Avenue. Also known as "The Bowman and The Spearman."

Lions by Edward Kemeys
1894
West entrance to the Art Institute of Chicago
Michigan Avenue at Adams Street
Grant Park

These two large male lions guard the main entrance to the Art Institute.

Monument to Johann Wolfgang von Goethe by Herman Hahn
1913
Diversey Parkway and Sheridan Road
Lincoln Park

A 25-foot idealized figure symbolizing the great German poet.

Nicolaus Copernicus by Bertel Thorvaldsen and Bronislaw Koniuszy
1823 (reproduced and installed 1973)
Solidarity (Achsah Bond) Drive leading to Adler Planetarium
Burnham Park

This 8½-foot-high representation of the noted Polish scientist was made by Bronislaw Koniuszy from Bertel Thorvaldsen's working model. The original 1823 sculpture made of plaster was destroyed in Poland during World War II.

Nuclear Energy by Henry Moore
1967
Ellis Avenue between 56th and 57th streets
University of Chicago

A compact 12-foot-high bronze sculpture that marks the spot where the first nuclear chain reaction took place.

Reading Cones by Richard Serra
1990
Monroe Street and Columbia Drive (temporary location)

A 17-foot structure consisting of two 16-ton pieces of steel.

The Republic by Daniel Chester French
1918
Hayes and Richards drives
Jackson Park

A 24-foot replica of the towering 65-foot "golden lady" that was chosen to symbolize the nation's progress since Columbus at the 1893 World's Columbian Exposition.

The Spirit of DuSable Sculpture Garden by Robert Jones, Ausbra Ford, Geraldine McCullough, Jill Parker, Ramon Bertell Price, and Lawrence E. Taylor
1963 (bust) and 1977 (other garden pieces)
DuSable Museum of African American History
740 East 56th Street near Cottage Grove Avenue
Washington Park

This sculpture garden features a 1971 bronze cast of a 1963 life-size plaster bust of DuSable, as well as five other sculptures added through a 1977 community development grant.

Stephen A. Douglas Tomb and Memorial by Leonard Wells Volk
1881
Douglas Tomb State Memorial Park
35th Street east of Cottage Grove Avenue

This mausoleum of the Democratic Party leader who ran against Abraham Lincoln supports a 46-foot column holding a nearly 10-foot bronze figure of Douglas.

Sundial by Henry Moore
1980
Adler Planetarium Entry Plaza
Solidarity (Achsah Bond) Drive, Burnham Park

Also known as "Man Enters the Cosmos," this 13-foot-high sundial consists of two bronze semicircles, one set inside and at right angles to the other.

Thaddeus Kosciuszko Memorial by Kasimir Chodzinski
1904 (relocated and rededicated 1978)
Solidarity (Achsah Bond) Drive leading to Adler Planetarium
Burnham Park

Originally located in Humboldt Park, this tribute to the Revolutionary War military leader of Polish ancestry was moved to Burnham Park in 1978.

Thomas Garrigue Masark Memorial by **Albin Polasek**
1941
Midway Plaisance east of Blackstone Avenue
Near Jackson Park

A 40-foot-high statue of a medieval knight on horseback
dedicated to the memory of Czechoslovakia's first president.

Ulysses S. Grant Memorial by **Louis T. Rebisso**
1891
Ridge Drive overlooking Cannon Drive
Lincoln Park

An equestrian look at Grant as the commander of the Union
forces in the Civil War. The horse and rider measure more
than 18 feet high.

Untitled Light Sculpture by **Hyong Nam Ahn**
1981
McCormick Place, Donnelley Hall Plaza
23rd Street and Dr. Martin Luther King, Jr. Drive

A 54-foot steel tower with 12 triangular steel panels, each
painted a different color.

Victory, World War I Black Soldiers' Memorial by
Leonard Crunelle
1927 (with figure of soldier being added in 1936)
35th Street and Dr. Martin Luther King, Jr. Drive

This column of white granite was erected by the State of
Illinois as a memorial to a regiment of black soldiers from
Illinois who died in World War I.

SUBURBS

Vita by Virginio Ferrari
1969
Loyola University Medical Center
2160 South First Avenue
Maywood, Illinois

A 24-foot-high sculpture and fountain consisting of two large wing-shaped bronze elements supported by a horizontal concrete cross.

COMMERCIAL MUSEUM-LIKE ATTRACTIONS

A number of Chicago-area attractions are not museums, but have some museum-like features. They include the following places:

Here's Chicago
163 East Pearson Street
Chicago, Illinois 60611
312/467-7114

Multimedia presentation on Chicago.

Six Flags Great America
P.O. Box 1776
Gurnee, Illinois 60031
708/249-1776

An amusement park.

SELECTED BIBLIOGRAPHY

Much has been written about Chicago's museums, galleries, buildings, public sculpture, and other arts and cultural activities. Some of the most helpful publications include:

A Guide to 150 Years of Chicago Architecture. Chicago: Chicago Review Press, 1985.

The Art Gallery Guide for Chicago and Vicinity. Chicago: Abstract Publishing, 1986.

The Art Institute of Chicago: 100 Masterpieces. Chicago: Art Institute of Chicago, 1978.

Bach, Ira J. (ed.). *Chicago's Famous Buildings.* Chicago: University of Chicago Press, 1980.

Bach, Ira J., and Mary Lackritz Gray. *A Guide to Chicago's Public Sculpture.* Chicago: University of Chicago Press, 1983.

Bollinger, Joyce, and Cindy Mitchell. *Have You Talked to Lincoln Lately?* Chicago: Friends of the Parks, 1976.

Chicago Gallery News. Chicago: Vol. 1, No. 2, Fall 1986.

Chicago Museums. Chicago: Chicago Council on Fine Arts, 1983.

Glibota, Ante, and Frederic Edelmann. *150 Years of Chicago Architecture: 1833–1983.* Paris: Paris Art Gallery and Musee Gelerie de la Seita, 1983.

Grant Park—Chicago's Front Yard. Chicago: Friends of the Parks, 1984.

Howarth, Shirley Reiff (ed.). *The ARTnews International Directory of Corporate Art Collections*. 1990–91 Edition. Largo, Fla.: International Art Alliance, and New York: ARTnews, 1990.

Kogan, Herman. *A Continuing Marvel*. New York: Doubleday & Company, 1973.

Krantz, Leslie J. (ed.). *The Chicago Art Review*. Chicago: Krantz Company, 1977.

Lincoln Park Map. Chicago: Friends of the Parks, 1984.

Loop Sculpture Guide. Chicago: City of Chicago Department of Cultural Affairs, 1990.

Maxon, John. *The Art Institute of Chicago*. London: Thames & Hudson Ltd., 1977.

Monuments and Memorials in the Chicago Park District. Chicago: Chicago Park District, 1979.

Museums of Chicago. Chicago: Museum Publications of America Inc., 1978.

Thomas, Bill and Phyllis. *Natural Chicago*. New York: Holt, Rinehart & Winston, 1985.

PHOTO ACKNOWLEDGMENTS

The photographs in this edition of *Chicago's Museums* appear courtesy of:

On pages 4–5, The Art Institute of Chicago; 8–10, the Field Museum of Natural History; 12–13, the Museum of Science and Industry.

On pages 19–20, Adler Planetarium; 22–23, Brookfield Zoo; 26, Cantigny; 27–28, Chicago Academy of Sciences; 30, Chicago Botanic Garden; 31–32, the Chicago Historical Society; 34–35, Chicago Office of Fine Arts; 38, Lincoln Park Conservatory; 40, Lincoln Park Zoo Society; 42, the Morton Arboretum; 44, Museum of Contemporary Art; 47, the Newberry Library; 49–50, The Oriental Institute, The University of Chicago; 51–53, John C. Shedd Aquarium; and 55–56, Terra Museum of American Art.

On page 63, Chicago Architecture Foundation; 64, Graham Foundation; 66–67, Frank Lloyd Wright Home and Studio Foundation; 70, Beverly Art Center; 72, Mary and Leigh Block Gallery; 75, the Martin D'Arcy Gallery; 77–78, Lizzadro Museum of Lapidary Art; 80–81, Museum of Contemporary Photography; 85, Renaissance Society; 86–87, David and Alfred Smart Museum of Art, The University of Chicago; and 94, Kohl Children's Museum.

On pages 96–97, the Balzekas Museum of Lithuanian Culture; 100, DuSable Museum of African-American History; 102, Mitchell Indian Museum; 104, National Italian American Sports Hall of Fame; 106, Romanian Museum of

Folk Art; 109, Spertus Museum of Judaica; and 112, Ukrainian National Museum.

On pages 116–17, Jane Addams' Hull-House; 122, Blackberry Historical Farm Village; 124, Des Plaines Historical Museum; 127, Dunham-Hunt Museum; 129–30, Ellwood House; 131, Elmhurst Historical Museum; and 132, Evanston Historical Society.

On page 134, Garfield Farm Museum; 135, Geneva Historical Museum; and 136, Graue Mill and Museum.

On page 138, Grosse Point Lighthouse; 140, Highland Park Historical Society Museum; 145, Illinois & Michigan Canal Museum; 151, Lombard Historical Society; 152, Morton Grove Historical Museum; 154, Naper Settlement; 155, Seven Acres Antique Village; 157, Paarlberg Farm; 158, Stacy's Tavern; 161, Western Springs Historical Society; and 163, Wilmette Historical Museum.

On page 168, International College of Surgeons; 174, Crabtree Nature Center; 178, The Grove; 180, Heller Nature Center; 181, Jurica Natural History Museum; 183, Little Red Schoolhouse; 185, North Park Nature Center; 188, River Trail Nature Center; 189, Ryerson Conservation Area; 191, Sand Ridge Nature Center; 192, Spring Valley Nature Sanctuary; and 194, Willowbrook Wildlife Haven.

On page 198, Bahá'í House of Worship; 200, Morton B. Weiss Museum of Judaica; 206, Fox River Trolley Museum; 207, Haeger museum; 208, Hartung's Automotive Museum; 210, Illinois Railway Museum; 212, Museum of Broadcast Communications; 217, American Police Center and Museum; and 219, Bradford Museum of Collector's Plates.

INDEX